My Storm, My Savior

My Storm, My Savior

Lessons Learned

Steve Moultrie

Strategic Book Publishing
www.sbpra.net

For information about special discounts for bulk purchases, please contact Strategic Book Publishing, Special Sales, at bookorder@sbpra.net.

ISBN: 978-1-68235-803-0

Dedication

This book is dedicated to the Glory of God and the furtherance of His Kingdom.

And, to my wife Julie. Her strength, resilience, and commitment to our marriage has been remarkable. Her courage has allowed this book to be in print. By putting aside her own feelings, she has allowed me to tell this story for the good of the Kingdom. From the day we met she has made me want to be a better man.

Acknowledgement

I would like to thank my dear friends and family who have read along with me as I have written. Your encouragement, thoughts, and corrections have been invaluable. Your fingerprints are all over this book!

Also, many thanks for the Devotion Staff at Wisdom Hunters: Boyd Bailey, Tripp Prince, and Shana Schutte. Their morning wisdom starts my day and gives me cause to live an examined life. The truths they share birthed many of the components in the Lessons Learned section.

Most of all, I give praise to the Holy Spirit for convicting me and inspiring me to put this on paper!

Hook ...

It's a Saturday morning in the middle of June. I'm in Publix supermarket and my phone rings. It's an old friend of mine and he starts the conversation with "Hey ... I just want you to know that me and you are good, and I don't know why I got chosen to make this call. So, please don't shoot the messenger ... but I've been asked to ask you not to attend the funeral on Monday."

Earlier in the week, one of my very closest friends passed away. I owed him money from a failed business. He and I remained friends, but he didn't want anyone to know. His family was very hurt, they are good people but didn't want me to be a distraction at the funeral. I understand. I deserve it. It hurts all the same.

Later that day, I was talking with a friend who also lost money in my fall. He asked if I was going to be at the funeral on Monday. I told him, "No, I was asked not to come and won't be there."

He responded by saying, "Man, I hate that, but I want you to know that if you outlive me, you will be one of my pallbearers. I told my wife." A friendship that transcends circumstances. Grace undeserved. Humbling.

Those two phone calls two hours apart sum up the extremes of my earthly existence over the last seven years. Scorn and disdain that I deserve. Grace and love that I do not deserve. Highs and lows, and lessons learned. I think I have a story worth telling. I hope and pray you will take the time to let me.

It is important for you to know as we go through this story that I don't fault anyone along the way for reacting strongly toward me. The people who invested in me and have not been paid back have every right to be mad at me. I realize that I can't create a situation and judge people based on their reactions to it. I will share my hurts along the way because you need to know the pain to appreciate the peace that I received.

Please know that nothing in this book is intended to make you feel sorry for me or cast judgment on anyone else. The hard feelings, I earned. The grace I did not. That's the thing about grace, the less you deserve it the more desperate for it you become.

Introduction

Most everyone has a story worth telling. And, for the most part, we like to hear those stories. I'm not talking about stories on Facebook or stories about a cross-country road trip. But real stories ... warts and all. Gripping stories that are hard to tell. The harder a story is to tell, the more important it is for it to be told.

The best church services I have ever attended were those that involved real-life people telling their real-life stories. Situations they found themselves in and needed divine help to get out of. Personally, that's where I learned the most about God's handiwork and man's molding to it.

People are curious by nature, and usually from a self-serving point of view. When someone dies, we want to know why in hope that we can bolster our own immortality: i.e., Joe was a smoker and died of lung cancer. I don't smoke, so I don't have to fear that form of demise. Sally had a bad wreck after a few drinks. I don't drink and drive, so I'm good. Currently, we want to know for certain if an acquaintance died *of* Covid or *with* Covid.

That powerful force of curiosity isn't confined just to our mortality. It's found in most every phase of life ... somebody's kid is always in trouble and we want to trace it back to some flaw in parenting, so we know our little Johnny won't end up on crack. The bad kid wasn't made to tuck-in and ours were, so we're good.

That curiosity within humans can be a great tool in revealing Christ to others, if we as Christians are willing to share our story. And by sharing it, I mean sharing ALL of it. For others to know how your faith sustains you, you must be willing to share just how far God had to bend over to lift you up out of the muck.

So, that's why I wrote this book. Because I have a story to tell about a storm that I am in, how God ministers to me, and to share lessons I have learned along the way. I decided I better write this now because my memory is fuzzy at best and will only get worse. Also, I don't have the option of waiting for my storm to be over. It will never be over, *but* I will never be alone in my storm.

As Christians, we are compelled to tell our story ... it's called our testimony. There is another truth that goes hand in hand with this. God never wants you to waste a trial or a pain. Sharing our experiences is how others can come to know Him and learn why it's important to have a relationship with Him.

In writing this, I must assume it will be read by people I have hurt, people who know me but don't know my full story, people who have walked alongside me during this and helped me greatly, people who have forgiven me, and people who just can't get there yet. I cannot stress enough that this is my storm; I own it. This book is not an effort to make you like me or feel sorry for me. The sole purpose of this book is to share in detail how in the darkest hours our Savior walks with us ... often carrying us along the way.

I also want to point out that this storm I'm referring to pales in comparison to the storms in other's lives that I have witnessed. I've seen friends lose children far too young. I've seen friends "lose" a child that is still alive yet living in a distant land as a prodigal son. I've seen friends lose their bouts with alcohol and drugs, people who have lost all hope and lost faith in the One who can get them through it. Some people are hurting in ways that I cannot imagine and can only ask that horrible question, "Why me?" My storm is a mess and filled with intense pressure, but I do not in any way proclaim to have "walked through the valley of the shadow of death."

How I Got Rich books are far more popular than "How I Survived Going Broke" books. Even though this deals with a financial storm, it's not a book about business. Willie Morris wrote a book about the recruitment and career of a star football player from Philadelphia MS called *The Courting of Marcus Dupree*. Morris said, "This is no more about football than Moby Dick was about fishing!"

I imagine good businessmen will shake their heads at my mistakes—I hope that young people starting out will learn caution—but most of all, I want everyone who reads this book to see the power of The Father, The Son, and The Holy Ghost.

Please have a seat and let me tell you my story ....

Contents

Chapter 1

Who I Am and How I Got Here

Some storms and stories come up rather quickly. Some are years in the making. The latter is the case with my storm. I can see the building blocks from an early age. Both the causes of the storm and the foundation of my faith that helped sustain me.

The things that matter in this book come later, the lessons learned and the power of God's hand in my life. However, to understand my storm you need to get to know a little about me, starting with who I am today.

First and foremost, I am a sinner saved and sustained by my Savior Jesus Christ. Some people will read this mainly to learn about my collapse and others will read it mainly for the lessons I learned. That fact in and of itself makes it hard for a novice writer—keeping a balance and not overloading you with mundane facts.

At the time of this writing, I'm sixty-one years old and an LED lighting contractor living in Guntersville, Alabama, five miles from Albertville where I was born and raised. In May of this year, I will have been married to my college (University of Alabama) sweetheart Julie Vandervoort for thirty-eight years. Much more on her later. We have five great kids:

- John is a physician in Atlanta married to Lauren. They have three boys, Wheeler, Reed, and Max.
- Paul is a business owner and real estate agent in Guntersville. He and his wife Allison have two daughters, Maggie and Rosie.
- McKinnon is a first grade teacher who lives in Guntersville. She and her husband Parker have two boys, Campbell and Cal.
- Sally is a doctor of physical therapy in Birmingham. She is married to her college boyfriend Jordan George.
- Sam, our youngest, is in his third year at the United States Naval Academy in Annapolis, Maryland.

As most parents are, Julie and I are very proud of our kids—I must remind myself that Mrs. Iscariot was likely very proud of her son Judas up to a point. Seriously, these are good kids who married well and, most importantly, have a relationship with Jesus Christ.

Sidebar ...

This fall, I read a story by Sean Dietrich telling about an event in his childhood at Christmastime where his father told him how proud he was of him. As it turned out, it was their last Christmas together. He closed the story by challenging parents: make sure your children know how proud you are of them. That struck a chord with me.

This year, between Thanksgiving and Christmas, I sat down and wrote a letter to each one of my children letting them know how proud I was of them. I listed character traits and events through the years that made me proud. It was an emotional thing to do and was very rewarding. It scared them though and they asked Julie if I was about to "go on in." I don't think I'm about to pass, but you never know! And one thing I know for sure is that when I do go, my kids will have no doubt how their dad feels about them. That is a very reassuring thought. I challenge everyone reading this: make sure that the people you love the most know just how much you love them—don't leave things unsaid. You will be leaving them an inheritance worth much more than silver or gold.

Life Before the Automobile Business

I am the fourth child of Bill and Cricket Moultrie. My siblings were Frank (eleven years older), Russ (nine years older), and Susan (six years my senior). Up until I was about twelve years old, my dad worked for NASA at Redstone Arsenal in Huntsville. Cricket was a stay-at-home mom up until I was fourteen. And by stay at home I mean stay at home. We only had one car and my dad drove it to Huntsville every day, except Thursday when he would carpool. So, all Mom's running around had to happen on Thursday—doctor visits, beauty shop appointments, grocery store shopping, you name it. If it didn't happen on Thursday, it didn't happen!

Growing up, because of the age gap, I don't remember much of my brothers other than being tormented by them and their buddies as a child. Ironically, I now co-teach a Sunday School class with one of those hoods who used to give me the business as a child. One of those guys gave me the nickname Mouse and it stuck. My old high school friends still call me that and it makes me smile. Susan was a great big sister and let me hang around with her and her friends, I'm sure more than she really wanted to. Looking back, I really appreciate that. Being a young boy and getting to hang around teenage girls was pretty cool.

I had a good, solid middle-class raising. Warm and safe and dry, a few miles outside of town on a forty-acre farm. Oddly enough, my parents never said "I love you" to me. But I never doubted it for a second. Maybe it was just something about that generation. Even in later years when I would get a birthday card or such from my mom it would always be signed "Love, Cricket." Just never could quite get that "I love you" down! What's even more amazing is the fact that it didn't send me off into some sort of awful dysfunctional state. I got messed up, but much later and not because of that.

I think raising Frank, Russ, and Susan took a lot out of my parents because when I came along they didn't seem to have the energy to inspire me to "be all I could be." I had rules and expectations for school but not much encouragement to play sports or get involved in extracurricular activities. I played baseball and basketball when I was young, but it was always a chore to get me to games and practices. I figured out later that we only lived four miles from town, but when I was young it seemed like town was on the dark side of the moon.

Work, however, was strongly encouraged. My dad couldn't stand to see me idle. After he retired from NASA, we raised cows and grew a large garden every year—perfect labor opportunities for a teenage boy. Any time he found me not busy, he got me busy. To the point that at age fourteen I rode my bike into town and found a paying job. My last two and half years of high school, I worked forty hours a week at Hewett Drug Store. I would go in at 7:45 a.m., work until 10:00 a.m. go to school for four classes, then return to work from 3:00 p.m. until 8:00 p.m. It was a great job but not a schedule that left much time to excel in my high school years.

I was raised in the First Baptist Church in Albertville. My parents were very loyal attenders and made sure their children were too—Sunday morning, Sunday night, Wednesday night, every week. I must admit at times it was a grind, but for the most part I enjoyed it and certainly learned a great deal about the Bible in the process. I accepted Christ when I was eight years old. Turning from my sinful past, I was baptized into the faith by Rev. Clinton M. Wood.

Growing up in the Baptist church, there was great emphasis placed on that moment of decision and "walking the aisle." I still recall that feeling, the urgency in my soul to step out into that aisle and walk down to the altar. Later in life, as I learned more of God and His Son, I began to question if my confession and Baptism were real. Did I actually know enough to make such an important decision? Our pastor came to our house, we sat down in the living room, and we talked it out. In the end, he assured me that what I felt earlier was real and, throughout my life, I would continue to learn more and more about Jesus and His nature.

What I didn't know then, but I do know now, is that salvation comes in an instant. Sanctification takes a lifetime and is never complete on this side of Heaven. That too is a reassuring thing to know.

When I became a Methodist after marriage, I had a hard time adjusting to their confirmation process. It makes sense to educate children and lead them to an honest conclusion about committing their life to Christ. But, it seems to miss that element of stepping out into the aisle all alone and making that walk down to the altar. I don't mean to get too far out in the weeds. I'm completely satisfied that my wife and children are bound for Heaven and grateful of that fact. Every day, I thank God for revealing Himself to me and my family. I pray that by His Spirit He will draw us closer to Him.

Our youth group at First Baptist Church was a very important piece of my puzzle. It helped me galvanize what I believed about Jesus Christ, and it gave me a venue for sharing my faith with others in a small and large setting. I believe the position of youth director is the most important job on a church staff. The twelve-to-eighteen-year-old range is tough. Kids are trying to find a place to fit in and figure out which way to go. If we as a church don't fill that void, then rest assured something else will. I was blessed to have a great youth minister and a great peer group. It helped forge the anchor I would need for my time at sea.

I finished high school in 1979. I mentioned earlier that my work schedule did not lend itself to a very active high school experience. Don't get me wrong, I enjoyed my years at AHS and had a great group of friends. Lifelong friends. However, as my senior year wound down, I became overwhelmed with regret. Regret that I didn't venture out and apply myself to being fully involved and strive to be a leader. I did very little toward "being all I could be."

To this day, I recall what a friend told me after our graduation ceremony, "Mouse, based on the way you walked across the stage and took your diploma, I'd say you get the 'I don't give a damn' award."

He was spot on. My body language was bad because I realized I had wasted the last four years. I vowed that day that I would not have that feeling again. I intended from that day forward to apply myself, get involved, and try to become a leader.

I was accepted into the University of Alabama (barely) and moved to Tuscaloosa in the fall of 1979. I pledged Sigma Chi Fraternity and was elected Pledge Class President. I got involved in campus politics and after being initiated held several fraternity offices including becoming president my senior year. I thoroughly enjoyed all the social trappings of college life and in December of 1983, I barely graduated.

I learned a great deal in college. Not much in class, but mostly about people and life. When you grow up in a small town, you basically spend your existence with folks just like you. Being in a fraternity forced me to live and work with guys from all over the US. Some more like me than I would have imagined and some very, very different. Adapting to that environment was extremely valuable for life. That setting forces you to analyze your beliefs and draw up a battle plan to defend those beliefs.

I became friends with people of great faith and people who made fun of us believers. Both groups aided me greatly. You can't really harden your beliefs in a warm, safe environment. You have to be called out, challenged on what you believe and why. Like I mentioned earlier, around home, there were a few bad apples but for the most part we all shared the same Christian beliefs— although we weren't always angels! In Tuscaloosa, I got to know Catholics, Jews, and flat-out heathens. All of which made me a better Christian.

The best thing that happened to me in college was meeting my future wife Julie Vandervoort in the fall of my junior year. I locked in and pursued her with everything I had. From day one, she made me want to be a better man and still does today. Her influence on my life showed up first in my academics. I mentioned we met in the fall of my junior year. By the calendar that was true, by my hours passed, I was still a sophomore. The more I grew to love her, the more I realized I had some catching up to do. I wanted to graduate, get a job, and get married in a timely manner so I piled on the hours and started taking school seriously. I even made it on to the Dean's List. From academic probation to the Dean's List! Quite a turnaround. All because she gave me purpose and urgency.

Winning her heart was my primary focus in life once we met. And I mean I worked it like Nick Saban going after a five-star recruit. Early on, when I would call her on the phone, I actually had notes because I didn't want the conversation to lag. I worked hard at being engaging. Just like in recruiting, when I got the chance to meet her mom and grandmother, I did my best to win them over as well. Bringing flowers to an eighty-year-old grandmother scores major points! I made sure that if Julie put me on the road, she'd have to answer to them.

One thing I learned along the way in my pursuit of Julie is that I could sell. I could win people over when I really focused on it. I came to understand that I could win trust easily—what I recognized to be my greatest gift, ultimately turned out to be my biggest enemy. Much, much more on that later.

I married way over my head. I know that and am often reminded by my "friends." My standard reply was "I had to go up the ladder; only girls in my peer group were in prison." We will talk more about Julie as the book goes on, but I must tell you now, right up front, that hurting her during all of this was the most painful thing I've ever experienced in my life.

I look forward to sharing with you her grace toward me and her resolve to our marriage. I wouldn't write this book without her permission because it puts our life on display for all to see. Sin and storms never happen in a vacuum. My kids and wife have been greatly affected by this trial of mine and laying it all out there will have an added impact on them as well. There is a lot of pressure to tell this story as God would have me to. They will learn things in detail that they did not know, and so will their friends and in-laws.

Anyway, back to the story at hand. In 1978, my father and brother Frank opened a Datsun dealership in my hometown of Albertville. They didn't have their building ready yet, so the first load of cars was delivered to our house. I came home from work and there were eight brand new cars sitting in our yard. Pretty exciting for a seventeen-year-old boy, especially the 260Z!

I was getting close to graduation and knew I needed a job. The family business was small and there really wasn't a place for me at the time and my father wasn't the type to create a job for his son and pay him money for nothing! Plus, I had a desire to see if I could make it on my own.

Fall of 1983 I bought a suit and began the interview process on campus. My major wasn't a great one (public relations) and my grades weren't stellar, but I had a lot of leadership and work experience on my résumé, and I could sell myself. I received a couple of offers and accepted a job as a sales rep for John H. Harland Check Company handling all the First Alabama Bank locations statewide. They weren't paying me a ton, but it was enough to check the last box I needed to ask for Julie's hand in marriage.

A little side story about my proposal. Being a southern gentleman and wishing to marry a southern belle, I had to request her hand in marriage from her father Hal. It was December of 1983 on a Saturday. I knew Hal would be out working on his farm, so I headed out to find him and ask his blessing. I found him in his barn and told him my intentions. He ran down a checklist and said he thought that we were ready. I thanked him and the last thing I said was "Please don't say anything to Julie, because she doesn't know yet." He told me not to worry, that he would "keep it under his hat." Apparently, he took his hat off when he got home!

About three hours later, I got a call at my parent's house (pre cell phones). It was Julie. She said, "Hey, do you have something you would like to ask me?" I played dumb and asked what she was referring to.

She replied, "Daddy just came home and said that we were getting married!"

That certainly broke the ice so I asked her if I could come pick her up and go for a ride. I proposed on the balcony of the

9

Lake Guntersville State Park Lodge overlooking the Tennessee River. She said yes and we began a wild, wild ride. However, I digress!

Harland was a great company to work for. I was in Birmingham, and that kept me close to Tuscaloosa where Julie was finishing up her RN degree. When I first started, I spent a couple of weeks in Atlanta and received some first-class training. I enjoyed what I was doing and saw a path to moving up. Because the branches were located all over the state, there was a lot of driving and I liked driving, especially when I got paid by the mile! I often wonder what life would have been like had I stayed with Harland or in essence, stayed out of the family car business.

Julie and I were married in May of 1984, and she came to live with me in Birmingham while she finished her preceptorship at Baptist Montclair. I like to tell people that I put her through college because we were married at the time she graduated. She doesn't let me get away with that though.

After about a year with Harland, I got a call from my brother Frank who was a sales rep for Nissan. There was a Nissan dealership for sale in Sylacauga, Alabama. He wanted to know if I would be willing to leave Harland and come to Sylacauga and help him run the store. The ownership would be my dad, Frank, John Mitchell, and myself. Twenty-five percent each and I would get a decent salary and a car to drive. How could I say no! And so began my life in the car business.

If I had only known then what I know now ...

Chapter 2

Life and Times of a Car Dealer

This chapter is intended to lay out my thirty-year run in the automobile business. It's meant to be a chronological account of my career and lightly hinting at the problems ahead and elements leading into it. Chapter three will reveal the storm in all its ugly glory, meant to somewhat overlay this chapter.

In 1984, we took over Bama Datsun is Sylacauga, Alabama, and changed the name to Spirit Nissan. Frank was the dealer principal, and I was somewhat of a finance manager. We had a good sales manager and a good service manager. Along the way, Frank opened a used car lot in his hometown of Birmingham and started spending most of his time there. I became the de-facto dealer and was as lost as I could be. Mind you, Frank had no retail experience either.

I think throughout my automobile career, my biggest deficiency was the fact that I wasn't a "car guy." In my opinion, car guys have a huge advantage. They *love* cars. When a car guy looks at an automobile, it looks back at him … they connect. They see its possibilities and remember most everything about it.

I wasn't in love with cars or fascinated by the car business. It was a product, a process, and a good opportunity. In my mind, a good businessman sees his best opportunity and runs with it. I studied all that was available to me and attended seminars to learn all I could. I didn't have the luxury of working with a mentor in the retail world. John Mitchell, a partner, tried but he was three hours away and busy running Moultrie Nissan in Albertville.

John is the best car guy I know and many share that same opinion. In 1986, John sold his interest in Spirit Nissan and, along with our accountant and Frank, bought a Nissan store in Enterprise, Alabama. Over time, John bought out his partners and masterfully wove his family into the business. This is an unbelievably hard thing to do ... and he makes it look so easy. He has since added several more franchises and does a fantastic job with all his stores.

When John moved to Enterprise, it opened the door for me to come back home and take his place. If you think it's tough being an expert three hours from home, try managing the people who watched you grow up!

Julie and I loved our time in Sylacauga. The people were very welcoming, and we have friends still today from the time we spent there. It was good for our marriage to be away from home and dependent on each other. It was a stressful existence but I'm not sure we realized it at the time. In our short time there, we welcomed our first child John and said goodbye to Julie's mom Ken.

Ken, named for her father Kenneth Earl Luckie, was the best mother-in-law a guy could ask for. She loved Alabama football and Braves baseball. She read the Birmingham paper cover to cover every day and could talk sports with the best of 'em. Ken fully supported me and, I'm sure, ran interference for me with Julie! Ken was diagnosed with lung cancer during the first year of our marriage and passed away after a brief bout with the disease. She was raised in Selma, Alabama, and was a charming southern lady through and through.

Julie and I have often talked about how our lives would have been much different had Ken lived a full life. Time has a funny way of changing your perspective. Julie recalls when her mother died, she rationalized that she had lived a good full life. At the time of this writing, Julie has outlived her mom by six years!

When we moved back north, we settled in Julie's hometown of Guntersville. We joined the church she grew up in, Guntersville First United Methodist, where we married. It's a great church that has grown in an unbelievable way.

The dealership was solid and steady but not wildly profitable. In its first seven years, I think the high-water mark for annual net profit was around $46,000. Knowing my dad, bigger profits might make you feel good, but they also meant more taxes. Mind you, I am about to start running a store in my hometown at age twenty-five with about fifteen months experience. I remember thinking at the time, in ten years, I will have seen it all and just be thirty-five years old. This is going to be great ... wrong. For one thing, ten years later, the car business looked nothing like it did in 1985.

When you marry over your head, move to your wife's hometown and home church, you must prove you belong. You have to step up! Remember the regret I felt over being a slug in high school? It was time to make up for lost time.

I dove headlong into the world of community service. In a short amount of time, I loaded my plate as follows:

- Albertville Chamber of Commerce Board
- United Way Campaign Chairman and President
- Formed the Albertville New Car Dealers Association and was its president
- Amsouth/Regions Bank Board of Directors
- Vantage Bank Board of Directors and a founding member

- Guntersville School Board (fifteen years)
- Marshall County Hospital Board
- Alabama Automobile Dealers Association Board of Directors
- Nissan Regional Advisory Board
- Southeast Toyota Advisory Board
- Organized 20 Men Who Care to meet needs of the children in Guntersville
- GFUMC—Trustee, Chairman of the Administrative Board, Sunday School Teacher, etc.
- Alabama Alumni Association Guntersville Chapter President
- 1994 Guntersville Citizen of the Year
- 2000 New Car Dealer of the Year for the State of Alabama

Getting involved and doing good work was very rewarding. I wanted to leave a mark on my community and make my wife and children proud. And, being involved in good things also helped folks feel good about buying cars from me, right? In retrospect, I have to dig a little deeper into my motives ... storm clouds gathering.

In 1998, Frank and some investors bought the Toyota dealership in Gadsden, thirty miles from the Nissan store in Albertville. In an effort to capitalize on our twenty years of advertising, it took the family name. Moultrie Toyota. Only one problem, the guy running the store did not share our same commitment to customer satisfaction. Early on, I began getting calls in Albertville from Toyota customers. Most of those calls were not pleasant. At one point, I told Frank that if his manager ever left, I wanted to run that store as well. There was too much at risk, too close to home.

Be careful what you ask for. About a year later, I was the executive manager for Moultrie Toyota. For thirteen years, this was my day: take the kids to school, open up the Nissan store at 7:30 a.m., spend a couple of hours there, drive the thirty miles to Gadsden, work there until 4:00 p.m. or so, then hit the Nissan store until closing time. It was a grind. I wasn't just on a treadmill, I was strapped to a rocket and had no idea how to get off.

The crew at Nissan felt neglected and rightly so. I was consumed with the Toyota store. It was a fresh start, a bigger market and a very hot product. It was invigorating to have a fresh start and big dreams. Over time, we bought out the other partner and owned it all: Frank at 55 percent, my brother Russell at 22.5 percent, and myself at 22.5 percent.

Russ has a degree in dentistry but did not enjoy his practice. He decided to get his MBA through the University of Alabama's Executive Program and upon graduation, took a job with Merrill Lynch. About the time he was finishing his training, the market crashed (around 1999). His manager told him his chances of survival were slim, so he left Merrill and joined Frank at the used car lot in Birmingham.

Dealing with Southeast Toyota (SET) was a different animal altogether. SET was retail driven to the max. No one worked in the field who hadn't worked in automobile retail. Direct opposite from Nissan. The pay pyramid was somewhat flipped where the reps in the field made very good money and were held accountable for their dealer's performance. If you weren't selling cars at the expected rate, they applied a great deal of pressure. Someone asked me the difference between my relationship with Nissan and Toyota. My reply was "Working with SET is kind of like working for the mob ... they're really in your business, but at the end of the day, the pay is okay."

We had some good months/years and, mostly, the profits went to buy out the "money man" who went in with Frank at the beginning. That was fine; we were building equity and had a franchise that was growing in value. However, we weren't gaining any ground in the cashflow department.

Along the way, another piece of the puzzle came about. Frank was able to acquire a struggling Ford store in Prattville, Alabama, and set-up a friend from the Gulf Coast as the manager. The store started to improve, and the Ford franchise made a big recovery. Suddenly, that store was a big commodity. But there was a problem. The articles of incorporation were a mess, and the operating agreement was as well. A long and costly lawsuit began over ownership percentages and control between Frank and his partner. More clouds.

After several years of running both stores, I conceded that I was spread too thin, and it was time to put all our eggs in one basket. Though thirty miles from home, Toyota had the most upside. It was our best bet to make things work. The plan was to completely focus on Toyota for a year or two and see if we could get it performing up to its full potential. If not, sell it as well and move on.

So, in 2012, we began to market the Nissan store, thirty-four years after its birth. It was sad. I'm thankful my dad didn't live to see that day. He passed away the year before at the age of eighty-seven. I'm so glad he didn't have to endure the sale. That was a blessing.

We had a few suitors, but in the end, Greenway Automotive was our high bidder.

They were a highly process-driven group based out of Florida that knew how to make money, branching out into smaller markets that they could dominate. We were their first Nissan store. They were good at what they did, but the way they processed a customer was somewhat different than the way we did it. One thing I was very pleased about was that they offered a spot to everyone on my staff. That made a tough situation a little better.

After a year or so, the writing was on the wall. Time to sell everything off, pay what we owe, and move on. The goal was to work hard to find the highest bidder and get out as soon as possible. When word gets out that you are selling, you better sell quick or there is hell to pay. In the next chapter I will fill in the blanks.

From a chronological standpoint this was how it began and ended. My thirty-one years in the automobile business covered by 1,943 words. That is *a* story but not *the* story. Time for me to cinch it up and tell you what you need to know about my storm so I can then tell you all about my Savior and my Sustainer.

Let's go ....

Chapter 3

The Fall

I might not have been specifically wired to run a dealership well, but I tried. I felt it was my best opportunity. I could sell and promote the brand and knew how to keep customers happy. But I did not manage people well to their fullest capacity. I had the mindset that "We are all adults here; you know what's expected of you, so go do it." Sounds fair enough but in the real world few people respond to that style of management.

I didn't demand enough out of the people who worked with me. I set goals and tracked them to a degree, but there was no real accountability for poor performance. Human nature holds a pecking order. If Joe is worse than me and Joe still has his job, then I'm okay. I let too many "Joes" just hang around and underperform. The truth of the matter is, by allowing that to go on, I was really the one underperforming the most! I had a car buddy tell me that the joke around town was "You'd have to punch Cricket Moultrie (my mom) on the showroom floor to get fired," which was not far from the truth.

I was an optimist. Even rare flashes of brilliance kept you employed. I also had a notion that the demons you knew about were often better than the ones waiting to hire-on. I liked safe and happy, but that's not how businesses grow and prosper.

People pleasers like me are great for customer satisfaction ratings but not so great for the bottom line. My theory was that, in a small market, you could not afford an unhappy customer. There is a lot of truth in that, but sometimes you need to draw the line and let some people walk away.

I think in all this, what I'm trying to say is that I wasn't good at doing the hard things to make our stores thrive. Don't get me wrong, we had success along the way and our factories loved us, but I didn't have the guts to do the hard things needed to go to the next level. Hitting that next level would have put us in a solid cashflow position and avoided the heartache I'm in the process of telling you about.

Let me tell you a sidebar here that really made me question how I was leading. One morning I had a sweet older woman come into my office. She was very humble and had a favor to ask. She said her son came in the night before and bought a car. She went on to say that he had "special needs" and didn't have the mental capacity to buy a vehicle. I told her I fully understood and would gladly tear up the paperwork—no questions asked. In the process of tearing up the paperwork, I looked at the recap sheet and discovered that we only made $200.00 profit on the deal! This guy without the mental capacity to buy a vehicle worked my team down to a $200.00 deal. Very disheartening.

The things listed above were impediments to my leadership ability, but I must say that my downfall was a result of pride, one of the seven deadly sins. I wanted to be man in charge, and I wanted to make it work my way. I didn't want my dad or Frank looking over my shoulder and I certainly didn't want to run to them with a problem. I longed for their approval and shouldered far more than I should have.

When I came to Albertville in October of 1986, our cashflow was adequate but not abundant. We had equity in property and personal assets so we were okay but never on easy street from a cash-on-hand standpoint.

The car business is a fickle mistress. She will tease you with good months and even years then cut you down to pieces just when you think you have her figured out. It's extremely sensitive to interest rates, politics, the market, and second only to farming concerning weather volatility. Face it, as an individual, you must feel really good about things in your world to go out and purchase a car.

For the non-car people reading this, let me explain how floorplans work and the importance of cashflow. The cars on a dealer's lot are owned by the dealer and financed by a bank. This is called a floorplan loan. When a dealership sells a car, they usually have three or four days to pay the bank off for that unit. That allows time for the dealer to get funded on the sale. Once a month, the bank comes to the lot with their list of cars they are owed money on. They check the inventory versus their list and verify what is sold. At that point, they want to be paid for what is sold. That is an elementary version of how it works. When they come to check the cars, it is called a floorplan audit. Floorplan audits were done without warning and became a dreaded part of my existence.

I hate to bog you down with all these details, but they are important to the makings of my storm. Floorplan audits reveal cashflow deficiency and all cashflow problems go back to lack of sustained profitability. It flushes out into the open a failure to address the problems at hand.

Another key element in my downfall was failing to act upon the cold hard facts that I knew to be true. Looking back on it now, I should've been brave enough or humble enough to step forward and tell everyone the truth. Truth number one: we could not sustain enough consistent profitability to support the number of people living out of this store.

I was too proud to say, "I can't make this work" or I was too scared. I was scared because I didn't know what else I would do for a living if my dad and brother agreed we were on a sinking ship. So, what did I do? I kept it all inside and began a cycle of borrowing money to keep things afloat. Each time I secured some breathing room, I rationalized it was affirmation I was doing the right thing. If I was good at anything in this world, I was good at borrowing money. Far too good for my own good and the good of those who trusted me.

I think now is a good time to share an important part of this story. I didn't create this storm all by myself. After we bought my dad out, the businesses were owned by me and my brothers. Along the way, I did shift away from keeping it all inside to involving them in everything I did and their obligations as partners. There is a temptation to add details concerning my partners' involvement in the storm. However, that could be interpreted as me trying to pawn my trials off on someone else. This is my storm. My partners are most definitely a part of it, but I want to keep the focus on the things I did and didn't do along the way.

In the previous chapter, I laid out a timeline of our years in the automobile business. Now I would like to highlight some of the events that flowed alongside those years.

My dad was in his sixties when I came back to Albertville and was ready to move toward retirement. Also, with estate planning, it made sense for him to sell the dealership to Frank and me. We paid for his portion over time from the Nissan store profits, and around 1991, Frank and I owned it—Frank sixty percent and me forty. I was the general manager and dealer principal.

Remember how early on I wanted to be "the man"? Well, I was, at the ripe old age of thirty-one. Being the man would cost me dearly some twenty years later. Being the man meant signing all the contracts and giving a personal guarantee. Being the man meant you were held accountable for all the corporate tax liability at the state and federal level. At the end of the day, being the man meant you got left holding the bag. The old saying goes, "It's lonely at the top." Well, let me tell you, it can be very lonely at the bottom when you are "the man."

Off and on, years of debt can resemble a high stakes game of musical chairs. Through the years there was a lot of "borrowing from Peter to pay Paul." I can honestly say that we didn't borrow any money that I didn't believe in my heart we could repay. We had equity in property, both business and personal, and I had the assurance of my partners that they would commit all they had to repay anything we owed.

Beyond the real property we could commit, the biggest asset we possessed was the value of our franchises, otherwise known as "blue sky." The only problem with an asset like blue sky is that the banks would not recognize that as a collateral asset. Banks could not loan money based on blue sky. That's an important piece of the puzzle that I will come back to.

For years, we worked within the traditional format to keep things rolling along. We had adequate profitability to sustain the stores—adequate but never solid. We survived but never really thrived. As I mentioned earlier, it took a lot to keep everyone up who lived out of the stores.

Moultrie Nissan eventually absorbed Hoover Motors, the used car store that Frank and Russ operated in Birmingham. We also became heavily involved in the wholesale car business, running hundreds of cars through the Nissan store each month. High volume and low profit margins were not good for the bottom line or cashflow. The "mothership" was getting strained.

Albertville-Marshall County is a unique car market: small in population for an import store and holding the distinction of having the most licensed dealers per capita in the United States. It's a used car mecca with a lot on every corner and hundreds of experts. Not exactly a recipe for success but we worked hard at making it work.

My friend Bob Hembree, a Chevrolet dealer in Marshall County said, "Being a car dealer is a hard way to make an easy living." There was a lot of truth to that. Very high risk, long hours, and huge liability.

We tried our best to play by the rules and treat people right. That was easy to do with a good moral compass but frustrating when you see your competitors cut corners and enjoy profitability without repercussions. But I digress …

Back to my point, we were making ends meet and hoping for better days. In 1998, Frank and some investors purchased a struggling Toyota store in Gadsden. The timing was good; Toyota was on the climb. As mentioned before, a couple of years later, I began running both stores, which split my time but also split my pay and gave Nissan some relief.

In a year or so, we were given the opportunity to buy out the main investor with profits over a period of time. This built our equity, but at the expense of not growing our cashflow. Eventually the store was owned by Frank, Russ, and me. This was helpful in the fact that we could rely on each other's fund's availability. And, by the way, I was installed as the executive manager for the Toyota store. I was now "the man" at both stores. What a mistake.

We were fairly well leveraged but making money and making headway up until the recession of 2008. The river ran low, and the rocks started to show. Our floorplan lender was Regions Bank and they immediately targeted automobile dealerships as a liability and started moving to discard dealers from their portfolio. Not just us, but many dealers were facing the ugly fact of having to go out into the borrowing market at a time when we weren't wanted. What really smacked in all this is that Regions took the federal bail-out money then kicked us to the curb. Frustrating.

BBVA-Compass agreed to take us on and we began a tumultuous three-year relationship. The people there treated us well, but they knew we were in trouble and made it clear we weren't wanted long term. These years were unbelievably intense.

The pressure to be profitable and keep everyone up over the last twenty years was tough. However, it paled in comparison to the pressure to survive and keep the doors open. Truth be known, we should not have survived 2008-2009. Looking back, I wish now that we would have crashed it back then. It would've been gruesome, but nothing compared to what lay ahead.

The thought of selling the stores at their lowest value point (during the recession) didn't make sense. We had to do all we could to make it to the recovery period then sell off to satisfy debt. That became the plan. We would do whatever it took to hang on until the blue sky values returned.

The banks had no interest in talking to us, so we were forced to look for other sources. Mind you, this is also a time when many people pulled out of the market and cash available on the sidelines, waiting on good times to return. Cash that was earning them little or nothing.

Let us stop right here and make one thing clear: I don't believe that making a return was the primary reason most people loaned us money in a time like this. I believe they did it because they trusted me and wanted to help. I will revisit this aspect of my storm a little later when I profile the people hurt by my collapse.

A key factor in this web is that, in 2009, Frank was able to gain access to a struggling Ford store in Prattville, Alabama, for no upfront money. He set up a friend as the manager and he turned it around. This became a huge asset in our portfolio, and we decided to cash it in to shore up the other stores.

Frank owned 51 percent of the stock. Or so he thought. As I mentioned earlier, the articles of incorporation were a mess and so was the operating agreement. This became a circus that ended up in court. Frank was trying to assert control to sell out and the manager was trying his best to prove his control of the corporation. This became an all-consuming fight and primary hope for our survival as the Ford franchise was now valued at over four million dollars.

Frank had attorneys in Prattville and I had good friends at home looking over our shoulder. When I say this was all-consuming, I mean ALL-CONSUMING. When we weren't in court or doing depositions, we were talking on the phone and talking to lawyers. We had to make this work at all costs.

His attorneys and my lawyer friends agreed we were in the right ... but, we had a problem. The judge in the case was a wild card. He didn't like Frank or his attorney. The hearings were brutal to attend as the truth made no difference at all. I lost all faith in our court system.

I was no longer a car dealer; I was Frank's de facto attorney. All day every day. I didn't enjoy it, but I had to do what I could do to help win this war. We spent a lot of money that we didn't have in this effort. It ultimately went to the Alabama Supreme Court and died there. Along with a huge piece of the puzzle for our survival.

With the Ford store sale dragging on and cash flow getting tighter, we were faced with the reality that we had to sell the Nissan store. It was sad but we had no choice. If we could get a decent blue sky price, that would buy us more time to get the Ford mess straightened out and let the Toyota blue sky value recover.

Seeing our family business that my dad started thirty-four years earlier go on the chopping block, on my watch, really hurt my heart. It was fortunate that my father didn't live to see it change hands. Deep down, I knew this was most likely a Band-Aid, but Compass made it clear that they wanted us gone and we had to position ourselves to streamline and be as attractive as possible for another bank.

The pressure to find another floorplan source in the midst of hard times was incredible. No floorplan meant closing the doors. Closing the doors meant losing the opportunity to sell the franchises. If a dealership shuts down for more than forty-eight hours, the manufacturer can take your franchise and award it to whomever they choose with no compensation to the current owner.

Borrowing money was a means to an end. That end being surviving until we could cash out at the top of the market. That was our only shot at paying everyone back. There wasn't really any hope of walking away with any cash. Just get everyone paid and move on. As the rat said, "Forget the cheese. Just let me out of the trap."

Bank of America became our only option to floorplan the Toyota store. They mainly believed in the Toyota brand and wanted to make inroads in Alabama at a time most banks were pulling away. It was a struggle to get approved. Frank was heavily invested in Florida property, which went south in a hurry. Bank of America had been involved in one of those deals so they couldn't include him in the approval process. Somehow, someway Bank of America took on our floorplan in August of 2012 and I was the personal guarantor.

We had a couple of floorplan audits that fall, and we survived. Meaning that after the audit, we sold enough cars during the grace period to cover what was owed on the audit. In February of 2013, they came in for an audit and it did not go well at all. The gig was up ... the music had stopped and there were not nearly enough chairs for everyone to have a seat. My prayer was that they would allow me to operate until we could find a buyer. They agreed and so began the worst two years of my life.

Bank of America came to visit and explained how things were going to be going forward. The bearer of this bad news was Canadian and spoke with a heavy French accent, which sounded more German to me, as in World War II German. I was now a prisoner of war, so to speak, and he was my commandant.

They would basically tie a bow around amount we were out of trust, meaning what we owed them for cars we had sold. And they would send in a person to oversee our day-to-day operations to protect their interest. In doing so, they laid claim to the first proceeds from the sale, but at least we got to keep the doors open until we sold.

Job one was to find the highest bidder and do so as soon as possible. Despite your best efforts, stores that are for sale don't do well in sales operation. Also, BOA was charging us an outrageous amount of money each month to oversee our store. Selling quick was very important, and selling to the highest bidder was very important. Those two things do not coexist well.

The term for my current position with Bank of America was forbearance. This basically meant they staked their claim to first funds from a sale and would oversee my operations until that happened. My other option would be them seizing my inventory, forcing me to close my doors and lose all blue sky value. So, I had no choice but to take what they offered me. During that time, I was reminded of a scripture:

> Very truly I tell you, when you were younger you dressed yourself and went where you wanted; but when you are old you will stretch out your hands, and someone else will dress you and lead you where you do not want to go.
>
> —John 21:18

I don't think I have spelled this part out yet. The most crucial reason that we had to get top dollar was because we had borrowed money from friends and family along the way to keep the wheels turning. Disappointing people at a bank is terrible, simply awful. Disappointing your dearest friends and family is unbearable. In the next chapter, I will lay out the details of that fallout.

I know this is somewhat out of context, but I need to reiterate something I mentioned earlier. This book is divided into two parts: The first part tells you the makings of my storm. Part two tells you the lessons learned and the sustaining grace I experienced. For part two to resonate with you, I need to make you feel the pressure and despair I experienced in part one.

Writing the first part is very difficult. It forces me to relive the darkest days of my life in painful detail. I'm ready to get through this part so I can get around to sharing the good part of the blessings I received, so let's get back at it.

Trying to sell something and trying to keep it quiet is virtually impossible and not fair to the people you employ. I viewed them as an asset, so I decided to make them part of the process. I think it was the right thing to do. However, human nature being what it is tends to shift the focus from the here and now on to the future. Ignoring the here and now gets expensive in a dealership.

The monthly losses started piling up. The Bank of America oversight fees were piling up. The value of the store was dropping by the month. The hope of a rescue from the Ford store was growing dimmer and dimmer. We needed a buyer and needed one right now.

I had reached out to several dealer associates and even enlisted a broker. I was seeking $6,000,000 for blue sky, parts, and equipment. That price would have gotten me very close to even. Especially if I could have gotten it early in the process.

In March, April, and May, we had several suitors but no firm offers. The bleeding continued along with the mounting pressure from all sides. Finally, in June I received a letter of intent to purchase from a Toyota dealer in south Alabama. It wasn't the six million I needed but it was the best we could hope for and it would mean a stop to the bleeding. The offer was $4.5 million plus parts and equipment would be just under five million. Not great, but not bad. It would mean a manageable shortfall if all went well. As you might have guessed, things did not go well.

My buyer backed out and never followed through on his agreement to purchase. Word had spread about the letter of intent and subsequent backout. Now I had damaged goods on my hands, much like a house that is under contract but fails inspection. Time was ticking and my bleed was now a full-blown hemorrhage.

A new buyer emerged. It was the same group that purchased my Nissan store a couple of years earlier. Their offer was four million and a discounted price on parts and equipment. I was out of time and had exhausted all options. I was instructed by Bank of America and Toyota to take the offer (or else). So I did and my buyer began the approval process … the long expensive approval process that carried us all the way through the end of 2013.

Having no control and no options, I got taken to the woodshed along with my creditors. The closing was set for early February. It was held at the dealership with the buyer's attorneys, the bank's attorneys, and Toyota representatives. I was there, but mainly as a spectator.

The buyer and Bank of America had a very strong working relationship outside of this particular deal. In what seemed to be an orchestrated move, the buyer reduced its offer by one million and the bank accepted it. They took the money, satisfied their portion and a couple of other creditors, and that was it. Nothing left over and nothing I could do about it. I had been led where it did not want to go. It was over.

I had spent a solid year being threatened, pressured, and cussed at. It was awful, but it was nothing compared to what was in store for me in the weeks and months to come. This was my storm and it was raging.

Chapter 4

The Fallout Part I: The Personal Side

Before diving into the fallout, let me flesh out a little of the numbers. In 2012, my partners and I had roughly eight million dollars in real estate equity and franchise blue sky. Eroding real estate value, lost litigation, and a forced fire sale gutted that eight million in a matter of two years. After the receiver in charge satisfied the secured creditors, there was nothing left. When my worst fears became a reality, I had to explain to my creditors the ugly truth one by one. My bankers and friends took a terrible hit and their blame rested solely on me. Letting these people down was my worst nightmare and all I could do was ask for forgiveness and hope one day that I could make some financial restitution beyond my inevitable bankruptcy.

Mistakes and sin never happen in a vacuum. They affect so many people in so many ways. I think I know the number of people I have hurt. Maybe, I can swing the pendulum and help more people than I have hurt. My hope in writing this book is that, first and foremost, God would be glorified by His standards and not mine, and people I have never met will be bolstered by my story. There might be someone reading this book who's in over their head and about to give up on life. If that's the case, I hope and pray that they will see in these pages that there is indeed life after failure—that Jesus Christ can sustain you and give you abundant life. Above all else, that is the truth I hope is seen in this book.

I want to share with you some of pain I caused people. People I love. People who loved me. Except for immediate family I won't call any names. People close to the storm will know who I'm describing and hopefully those not as familiar will still be able to follow along.

Bankers. I hurt several bankers who are/were good friends. One is related to me by marriage, which carries an even greater pain. Some I attend church with and even shared in an accountability group. These are good businessmen who let down their guard and lost money.

One situation was particularly embarrassing. In my hometown, a group of men and women were forming a new bank and asked me to participate as a founding board member. It was a great group of folks. I enjoyed the process of starting a bank and getting to know the people involved. As things began to unravel, I knew that there was an increasing risk that this new bank was going to take a hit. As the bank grew and each milestone was celebrated, I feared in the pit of my stomach that I was going to become a blight on this group. And I was. Ultimately when it was time to face the music, I resigned and asked their forgiveness, which I undeservingly received.

Friends. I let down childhood friends, fellow church members, the very people closest to me. As I mentioned earlier, people with money sitting on the sidelines were looking to invest in something to earn interest. I offered that, paying eight to ten percent in some cases. Paying that much interest in a recession is a race that you just can't win. Desperate men do desperate things. Some of my creditors may have made this risky decision based on promised returns, but I think that most made their decision based on their belief in me and a willingness to help. It still hurts knowing I let these friends down and I guess it always will. Many of these friends have extended forgiveness my way; others I sense can't quite get there and I understand.

Another casualty in my downfall was my witness and service within my church. I had been in some sort of leadership role for thirty years and serving in our church was a very important part of my life. That came to a screeching halt. Outside of the members who knew firsthand, there were countless others who knew enough to know it was bad.

I went to see my pastor and told him I needed to step down from my position as chairman of the staff parish committee. He didn't ask why or ask me to stay on, so it was safe to assume he was in the loop. He asked if I was going to leave the church and I told him no. As hard as it was to stay, I knew we had to. Going forward, I made it a point to avoid the services and activities that would put me around those I had hurt. I knew that the sight of me would be a stumbling block for their worship. I made every effort to stay in the shadows as best I could.

In the grand scheme of things, the damage I did to my witness is truly the worst thing about all this mess. This book is a byproduct of that pain. I know I'm forgiven. I know I have repented. The third thing is I must be obedient in sharing my pain for the good of the Kingdom. It's the only thing I can do to attempt to repair my witness. I have to bare it all if I hope to, one day, help more people than I have hurt.

Family. I mentioned earlier that one of my bankers was a family member of mine by marriage. A situation like this can't help but put a strain on a relationship. Time heals but I'm still sensitive to the trouble I caused by not being able to fulfill my obligations. It takes a lot of grace to move beyond the disappointment and try to maintain family peace. I'm grateful that I've been extended that grace, undeserved as it is.

Our sister took a huge hit in all this as well. Much of her inheritance was tied up in assets that we leveraged along the way. She trusted us to take care of her part and we didn't do a good job of doing so. She was hurt, mad, and didn't understand how we could be so reckless. And rightfully so. She has extended unmerited forgiveness, which is a testament to her faith and character.

My children. Children are forced to pay for the sins of their father. It's biblical and it breaks the father's heart when he sees it. Our kids are spread out over fifteen years, so they were in varying life points when all this was unraveling. Our oldest, John, was married and doing his residency in Kansas. He was somewhat removed and witnessed less of the fallout.

Paul was back in our hometown and trying to establish a business. Undoubtedly, he was put under undue scrutiny because of who his father was. Also, he had friends who were the children of those who lost money. At one point along the way, he entertained the idea of working at the dealership and even did so for a while. I never really embraced that idea because I feared in my heart it was a sinking ship.

McKinnon was back home working and most likely the most in-tune. Guntersville is a small town and holds few secrets. She felt the cold shoulders and no doubt heard the bad news more than the others.

Sally was finishing high school. She too had friends whose family took a hit. Very close friends. She also had to sense the fear of living in a financially unstable home. Her college experience was going to be much different than the other kids. Much of her college was funded by student loans, grants, scholarships, and odd jobs. She survived and thrived and probably came away a better person for it.

Sam was twelve years old when things bottomed out. I don't really know to this day how much he realized or internalized what was going on around him. His parents' relationship was strained, and the financial cloud dictated everything we did and didn't do. No doubt he knew enough to have his foundation shaken. He was motivated throughout school to excel in academics and track. I have often wondered if that motivation stemmed from a desire to earn a scholarship and take some pressure off his parents. If so, I feel guilty but at the same time, very proud. Sam earned an appointment to both West Point and the Naval Academy. When he walked through the gates of the USNA, he was 100 percent on the payroll of the U.S. Navy. That financial relief has certainly been a blessing.

My wife Julie was by far hurt the most. In so many ways. I was wrong to keep her in the dark for so long. When the truth started to spill out, she was devastated. She questioned how the man she knew so well and loved could have kept so much from her. I kept secrets that would ultimately destroy her friendships and strain family relationships to a breaking point.

Julie knew that I was constantly under stress from work but didn't know the extremes I went to in keeping all the balls up in the air. To fully understand her hurt, you need to understand a little about her. She is very thrifty. She is a rule follower. She values the importance of a good name in your community. She balances her checkbook to the penny and always has. She is "buttoned up." Some would like to think that this was some sort of Bonnie and Clyde, but I can assure you, Julie was no Bonnie.

Late in the game, when we needed more cash to survive while trying to sell the Toyota store, I approached her brother about borrowing some money from a bank he was associated with. As I struggled to make it work, they needed collateral. With her brother helping to put it all together, Julie's fourth of the family farm became that collateral. That portion of her inheritance was lost by my recklessness. She has often said, "I should have asked more questions. I could have stopped some of this long ago." She trusted me and I let her down terribly.

To make matters worse, our home was built on land that we purchased from her father. That purchase was made with proceeds from the sale of her mother's farm in Dallas County. We had to sell our home to avoid foreclosure prior to my bankruptcy. So, in this collapse, Julie lost her inheritance from both her mother and father. She lost a precious part of her heritage because of my mistakes.

It is ironic that some people blame her and have identified her as my accomplice. Nothing could be further from the truth. The scorn she faced because of my actions is my greatest pain. I not only let down the woman I love but I forced her into a spotlight that she did not deserve.

Let me tell you about the worst day of my life. Earlier in that week, my accountant and great friend asked me to stop by his office. With all the love he could, he told me that talk was getting around town about my troubles and that I really needed to come clean with Julie. I knew he was telling the truth and doing so from the standpoint of a Christian brother and friend. But the truth was going to be so hard to tell.

I gave it a shot. I wanted to tell enough to satisfy my guilt, but not so much that she would hate me. I mean, the store was still for sale and there was still a chance that things might be okay … right? Wrong! I told her some of what had been going on but didn't paint the whole picture. That was a terrible mistake.

We had been out of town on a Chamber of Commerce trip. The day we were coming back, her brother called and asked her to stop by his lake cabin. She assumed that meant both of us and most likely was something to do with the loan and farm. As we got closer to home, he let her know that it would be best if she came alone. I knew where this was headed. This was a gut-wrenching intervention, and I was the drug.

We got home and she left to go to the cabin. She returned devastated. What she had known faintly, she now knew in full detail. Her family had been putting all the pieces together and, rightly so, laid it all out for her. I don't think I'd ever made Julie cry before. It broke my heart to see her so crushed and to know it was all my fault. It literally makes me sick at my stomach to be writing these words. These last few paragraphs were my biggest barrier to writing this book. Reliving that Sunday afternoon breaks my heart all over again. I hope you can catch just a fraction of the pain I caused and felt. It's important that you do, because if you do, you can also feel some of the grace I have received from the person I hurt the most.

Chapter 5

The Fallout Part II: The Business Side

Once all the assets I had control over were sold, there was a mountain of debt to deal with. I was the managing partner and sole personal guarantor on most of the debt. So, computer systems, bank loans, tax liability, etc., fell on me.

Consequently, I began the inevitable task of filing for bankruptcy. The legal process of bankruptcy is tough in and of itself. There was also pressure leading up from people wrangling for better positioning in the fallout. For instance, I was asked to give an affidavit professing something to be true that wasn't. The request came with a threat as to what would happen if I did not oblige. I declined. If I had learned anything at all through this, it was that, from this point forward, my yes was yes and my no was no. No more letting the end justify the means. I was in enough trouble and wasn't going to tell a lie no matter what. That decision cost me a lifelong relationship. It hurt then and hurts today, but if healing were to ever happen, it had to start then and there.

Nobody wins in a bankruptcy, at least no one who goes about it in an honest fashion. I suppose the purpose of bankruptcy is to make sure no one leaves with an advantage. Seems like the courts view a loan as a business partnership and when it goes south, their job is to make sure the debtor doesn't walk away with any assets that should be used to satisfy the debt. The partners must suffer equally from the failed venture. People on both sides fall into this saying, "All lost some, some lost all."

My creditors were relegated to pennies on the dollar, and I lost all my assets. To this day, the only asset I own is a ten-year-old Toyota Tundra with 512,000 miles on it. I am so blessed that it's still running. I am thankful and recognize it for the miracle it is.

Leading up to submitting a bankruptcy plan, attorneys for the creditors were allowed to take depositions and fully examine all my financial documents. My life was laid bare. Obviously, their intent is to locate any hidden assets to bring to the table. What they found was that I had put everything I had (and then some) into keeping the business afloat until it could sell. I had nothing left.

The hearings leading up to my plan being submitted and approved were hard to sit through. And rightfully so. I deserved it. I would drive to the federal courthouse in Anniston, briefly meet with my attorney, then sit in the crowd waiting on my case to come up on the docket. That courtroom was a sad place to be. You witness person after person standing broke and broken in front of a judge begging for relief. It seemed surreal to be one of those people, but I was … and because I did such a poor job of spreading the blame around, my case probably set some sort of record.

My judge seemed like a fair and caring person. He didn't lecture or look down his nose at those of us before him. If he had a stipulation to administer, he did it much like a father would to a child. He seemed to have a mixture of grace with his law. About halfway through my plan, I ran into my judge while visiting family in Anniston. I introduced myself to him and told him I appreciated his respectful manner in the courtroom. He didn't remember my case but thanked me for my kind words. It's nice to see someone with such power going about his job with compassion.

It's also odd to listen to the lawyers discuss you in front of the judge. Kind of like overhearing your parents discussing something you've done or said. It is like being that proverbial "fly on the wall" as your past and future are discussed.

After several months of wrangling and lawyering, my plan was submitted and approved. The IRS and State of Alabama were considered preferred creditors and they would receive 100 percent of what was owed: $202,000. This was sales and payroll taxes that we attempted to pay but the bank in charge did not allow it. I took on all that debt as the managing partner. The other creditors would receive $130,000. It was a small amount of what they were owed. Like I said, nobody wins in a bankruptcy.

The plan would give me sixty months to satisfy the obligation to the creditors. Roughly $5,600 per month and I had to produce enough to live on during that time. Fortunately, Julie had begun working for the local school system prior to the fall. She didn't make a ton of money, but had outstanding insurance at a great price. That preemptive grace, her taking that job, has meant a great deal to us financially over the last few years. Fortunately, Julie didn't have to join me in my bankruptcy. As I mentioned earlier, she lost her home and her inheritance, but at least she was spared the injustice of having to file bankruptcy.

Another key factor in this financial fallout was the fact that I wasn't going to have a job anymore. And, having "bankrupted a Toyota dealership" on your resume was not very attractive. I needed a job, a good paying job, in the worst way. God provided for me with one phone call. This will be addressed in greater detail later on, but let me just give you the basics for right now. I had a customer named Joey Gilliland. I wasn't exactly sure what Joey did but I knew it was poultry related and I knew Joey was very good at it. He was the one and only call I made. The call went something like this:

Me: "Hey Joey, this is Steve Moultrie. How are you doing?"

Joey: "Hey Steve, I'm doing good."

Me: "I'm getting out of the car business and am going to need a job. Do you have anything going on that you might need some help with?"

Joey: "Matter of fact, I do. I think I need to be in the LED light business and need someone to take the ball and run."

As I said earlier, much more on that miracle later. I had a mountain to climb, but I had been given an opportunity. I had hope. I also had the reality of knowing that I would spend the rest of my days trying to pay back the people I owe. I will never retire; I will never have an asset in my name or any money in savings. All I can make will go toward living a conservative life and paying debt. My obligation to these folks goes beyond what the courts say I must pay. That's why I say that my storm will never be over, but I do have a Savior who sustains me in my storm.

So, we have covered who I am, the makings of my storm, and the fallout of my poor decisions. I have tried my best to let you feel my pressure and my disgrace. It's important for you to get that picture. I was on rock bottom; at the bottom of a well. Financially, I lost it all and my marriage was at a breaking point. The family I grew up with was splintered and my children's world was shaken at its core. You have to understand this depth to fully appreciate the things I'm about to share with you concerning my Father, His Son, and the Holy Spirit.

Lesson 1

Dreading the Worst-Case Scenario Can Be Worse than Living It

It is the Lord who goes before you. He will be with you; he will not leave you or forsake you. Do not fear or be dismayed.

—Deuteronomy 31:8

For His eye is on the sparrow, so I know He watches over me.

I lived in dread of my worst-case scenario for a long time. Even when times were good. In varying degrees, I lived with a deep-down gnawing of an impending failure. Later as the storm raged, the vision of letting family and friends down was gripping and unimaginable … I just couldn't let that happen. I fought tooth and nail to avoid it, but alas, I did not. And in the end, the harder I had fought against the inevitable made the result even worse.

Lesson: The dread is worse because your mind can't factor in the many ways Christ ministers to you when your worst-case scenario becomes your reality.

I come from a long line of worriers. I think it is in my family's DNA. Worry tormented my mother her entire life, which mainly manifested in health scares and bad weather. The funny thing about her is that her propensity to fret did not render her down or depress her. Or, maybe she just put up a good front around her kids, kind of like her son Steve.

My dad, however, was the whole package! He worried and dreaded with the best of them and shared his woe with all those around him. When the sky was falling, he knew it and made sure you did too. From the outside looking in, he had nothing at all to worry about. He was financially secure, in good health, and had no relational strife. However, there was something in his make-up that prevented him from being fully at peace. I always felt sorry for him because he couldn't fully enjoy the blessings that surrounded him. I tried my best to help him recognize the things that should bring him peace, but he just couldn't completely get there in his heart and mind.

We are all wired with something we must overcome to fully live the life God intends for us. For some it is addiction, some greed, some sexual sin, some envy ... you name it. But for some, it is simply worrying too much about what you think or know might be on your horizon.

I think the thing that bothers God about our worrying is that worry reveals a lack of Faith. Worry makes this statement: "I'm not sure God has what it takes to see me through what lies ahead." Worry calls into question God's ability to sustain us. When you look at it from that standpoint, worry goes from benign human trait to an affront to the Most High! Worry and dread are sins to be dealt with just like lust and greed. Fear of a worst-case scenario is a barrier to a life fully lived as intended by our Creator.

Looking back on things now, I wonder if some of my uneasiness was less worry and more the feeling that, where I was really wasn't where God intended me to be. Time and time again, I found myself in settings that just didn't feel right. Not in a sinful manner, but an awareness that I was a square peg in a round hole. Deep down I knew being a car dealer wasn't my destiny and deep down I knew getting blasted out of that role was going to hurt. It did. It hurt me and many around me.

Please don't get me wrong. There are plenty of unpleasantries about where I am today, but the power of the Holy Spirit sustains me in ways I could not imagine during my days of dread. Every morning, I praise God for the gift of His Son on the cross and the gift of the Holy Spirit, and I thank Him for forgiveness for my past, hope for my future, and peace for my present, through the Blood and through the Spirit. When you earnestly seek those gifts, they become a very real part of your day. You can't fathom having any form of peace or hope while you are in the midst of dread.

Putting up a good front while fearing what lies ahead is exhausting. Having to be "on" all your waking hours at work and at home wears you out. And by being "on" I mean either trying to plan your next move or putting on a happy face, so no one sees you sweat. That was how I lived for way too long. Don't get me wrong, my days are still full of stress, but they are lived out in the open with no secrets gnawing away at me.

There is so much truth in "The truth shall set you free." When I finally gave in and decided to be obedient and write this book, a liberating peace filled my soul. Once this is finished and my mistakes are available for all to see, then the shame, hiding, and dread are over. God can't really be glorified amid dread. However, He can be glorified in the presence of truth.

Coming clean, entering your new reality, and leaving your dread behind strips away so many energy drains that held sway over you. People and things that held you captive go away and leave room for the more important things in life, things that bring quality to your life. I was sitting in a waiting room the other day, scrolling through the contact list on my phone. One after the other, I looked at a name and remembered the anxiety induced when that person popped up as an incoming call or email. The reason for the anxiety varied but it was all very real. Once the cards were on the table, at least that part was over. Janis Joplin sang, "Freedom's just another word for nothing left to lose ..." In my world that line rings true as "Freedom's just another word for nothing left to dread."

Granted, you must live with the hurt you caused but at least it's in your present and not your future. You fully know what it looks like and what it feels like. You know how people took the news, good and bad. Working toward restitution and reconciliation is much more meaningful than dreading a day of reckoning and being crippled by those thoughts. Realistically, full restitution isn't likely. However, reconciliation can occur with Christ's help.

I have a whole chapter later about earthly grace I have received. It's humbling and has brought me to tears. See, you just can't imagine that when you are in the grip of dread. Living in grace from above and grace from fellow man washes away so much of the pain you imagined leading up to your new reality.

I'm not exactly sure that this chapter is the best one to include this story, but it's worth telling even if it's a stand-alone lesson.

Paul and Jolynn Claborn are two very dear friends of mine. Lifelong friends. A couple of years ago, they tragically lost their only son Warren at the age of twenty-one. Warren was a great kid and the apple of his mom and dad's eye. They poured their heart and soul into his upbringing. He was raised right. His passing was heartbreaking and devastated our entire community and many people beyond.

Warren's celebration of life was an amazing event. Hundreds attended including busloads of Warren's friends from college.

During the service, Paul spoke of the great qualities of his son. An incredibly hard thing to do, I can only imagine.

During Paul's talk, he spoke of how, as a businessman, he spends so much of his time trying to be prepared for whatever may come his way. He shared with us that there was no way in the world he could have prepared to face this tragedy. Sadly, I agreed with him. He and Jolynn are living every parent's worst nightmare.

A couple of days later I was having my morning prayer time and was lifting up the Claborns. The Holy Spirit spoke to me a truth that I, in turn, shared with Paul as follows:

Paul,

I respectfully disagree with you stating that you were completely unprepared for this tragedy. I understand what you mean, but I would like to point out that you were infinitely prepared.

Number one: You made sure that you had a vibrant relationship with Jesus Christ. You know Him well and you have Him to lean on.

Number two: Most importantly, you made sure that Warren was raised in church and in a Christian home. You made sure that he too had committed his eternity to his Savior, Jesus Christ.

Number three: You have plugged yourself into a community of strong believers who are capable and willing to lift you and Jolynn up and help sustain you during this time of loss.

You may not have realized what you were doing at the time, but the reality is, you were preparing you and your family for whatever this world had to throw at you. Please take comfort in that.

Love,
Steve

Now, let me be perfectly clear. In no way, shape, or form am I comparing my storm to the storm Paul and Jolynn are enduring. No comparison whatsoever. However, no matter what storm is on your horizon, you must prepare the same way to survive.

- Have an intimate relationship with Jesus.
- Make sure your family does as well.
- Surround yourself with committed believers.

Strive to replace worry and dread with these tenants of your faith. Work hard to stay out of life's storms when possible but embrace a calm assurance that your faith is well placed. Develop an abiding walk with Jesus and you will be prepared for the worst!

I didn't figure out a way to avoid what I so dreaded. I see now it wasn't God's Will for that particular cup to pass, but thankfully, I had done the things I could do to survive it. Praise God from Whom all blessings flow ... even in the midst of life's storms.

Application:

What's going on in your life that's causing you dread and worry? Resolve today to face the brutal facts and address it. Once you do it, you will begin the journey to freedom that only comes from the truth!

Lesson 2

Whose Storm Is This Anyway?

And His disciples asked Him, 'Rabbi, who sinned, this man or his parents that he was born blind?' Jesus answered, 'Neither this man nor his parents sinned, but this happened so that the works of God would be displayed in him.'

—John 9:2-3

The sailors were afraid and each cried out to his own god. And they threw the ship's cargo into the sea to lighten the load. But Jonah had gone down to the lowest part of the vessel where he lay down and fell into a deep sleep. The captain approached him and said, 'How can you sleep, get up and call upon your God. Perhaps this God will consider us so that we may not perish.'

—Jonah 1:5-6

Lesson: no matter whose storm it is, if you are aware of it, as a Christian, you have a role in it.

The Bible is full of stories about storms at sea. I heard them as a child and could picture the raging seas and howling winds. Living here in the south, we understand what a storm is and can easily understand the metaphor tying them to life events.

Growing up in Sunday school every week and, of course, hearing countless sermons, I knew the story of Jonah inside and out ... or so I thought. While my own storm was raging, Julie and I were taking a Wednesday night class on the Book of Jonah. Suddenly, it hit me. Most certainly, the storm that overtook the boat was Jonah's storm, *but* the others on that boat were certainly a part of the storm and story! What a revelation. That in and of itself is a lesson on the Living Word of God! I have heard and read that story hundreds of times and never thought about the others in the boat.

The literal storms in the Bible have purpose. They are used for correction, such as the case with Jonah, to glorify God and as a test of Faith.

Suddenly a violent storm came up on the sea, so that boat was engulfed by the waves; but Jesus was sleeping. The disciples went and woke Him saying, 'Lord save us! We are perishing!' 'You of little faith,' Jesus replied. 'Why are you so afraid?' Then He got up and rebuked the wind and the sea and it was perfectly calm.

—Matthew 8:24-26

Though the disciples had been with Jesus for some time and seen many miraculous things, they didn't fully trust in the power and security he offered. We shouldn't be too hard on the disciples; after all, don't we often fall into the same category. We ask for Jesus's help but don't fully expect Him to be the answer. Yet, after the storm dies down a little, we look back in amazement much like the disciples did.

Just like the examples in the Bible, storms in our lives today have a purpose. You might be in the very heart of the storm. You might be so close that you too are drowning. You might be watching from the shore, or you might be learning about it in a

49

book right now, hearing a distant roll of thunder. Storms test the character of the owner of the storm … of the shipmates and of the observers on the shore.

Hopefully, you can stop and reflect on a storm you either endured or one you are awaiting. Below are some thoughts about the possible impact from my storm in particular:

- Maybe my storm changes the course of one of my kids who internalizes a valuable lesson and lives their life differently because of it.
- Maybe my storm puts on display the resilience of my wife and in turn inspires another wife to ride out the storm in her marriage.

For if you forgive men's trespasses, your heavenly Father will also forgive you. But if you do not forgive men their trespasses, then neither will your Father forgive yours.

—Matthew 6:14-15

Maybe you have been hurt deeply by someone's storm. If so, it tests the depth of your forgiveness. I didn't want to include this part because of my fear that it comes across as self-serving, as if I'm trying to shame someone into forgiving me for the things I did. Certainly, I do crave forgiveness and reconciliation, but that is between them and God. As with all scripture, I believe the passage above to be true. It carries a stern warning but also the tremendous blessing of peace.

I have spent a fair amount of time helping in jail ministry and addiction recovery programs. There is a recurring theme and base root problem of an inability to forgive either someone close or, in most cases, themselves. It's not necessary to be restored to the people who hurt you. You don't need to put yourself in a position to be hurt again. You do, however, need to ask the Holy Spirit to bring you to the point where you can truly forgive and be set free.

Maybe you were on the fringe of a storm and have a relationship with the people getting battered about. If that's you, don't underestimate the importance of your role. Little things mean so much in hard times. Calls, texts, cards, visits, etc. They mean the world when you are hurting. It's a hard thing to do, kind of like going to a funeral home. But let me ask you this … have you ever regretted going to the funeral home? Don't you always leave feeling glad you reached out to a hurting friend and know that they know you care?

You never know how far little things can go. As I mentioned earlier, a gentleman that I didn't know well said one day, "I'm not really sure what all you are going through, but the way you and your wife are handling it surely is a testament to your faith." Those were very encouraging words. But when he said them, I doubt he knew what the long-term effect would be. A light went off in my mind. Up to that point, I had hoped that as few people as possible would know of my plight. In that moment, the Holy Spirit revealed unto me this truth. God can't be gloried in this storm if no one knows about it. I was wasting a pain by trying to save my pride. That kind statement, followed by the Holy Spirit's revelation, has led me to write this book. I want God to be gloried by His standards, not mine.

Maybe you were a complete stranger to my storm until you picked up this book. I want you to know something. You are the main reason I'm writing this book. Let me tell you what I'm going to do if this book makes it to print. This may appear to be a selfish endeavor, but I hope to use this one day to make a visual point as to God's blessings that flow from obedience.

I'm going to get a ledger and a folder. In the first pages of the ledger, I'll write all the names down of those who were hurt in my fall. In the following pages, I hopefully will be able to write down names of people who let me know that they read this and learned something of the nature of Jesus Christ. My hope is that one day the names of those helped will outweigh the names of those hurt. God has written a story upon my heart and compelled me to share it for His Glory. I pray it makes a difference for the Kingdom!

This is pretty random but I can't get it out of my mind. While writing about storms and shipwrecks, the gospel hymn "Love Lifted Me" keeps coming to mind. It's one of my favorites from days growing up in First Baptist Church in Albertville. Do yourself a favor and Google Jack Black sings "Love Lifted Me." You will be glad you did! Also, if you haven't seen the movie *Bernie*, which this clip comes from, I highly recommend it as well.

Application:

Earnestly pray today and every day that the Holy Spirit would open your eyes to the storms going on around you. Pray that He would inspire and equip you to fulfill your role in that storm to His Glory!

Lesson 3

Grace So Precious, So Undeserved

Therefore, let us draw near with confidence to the throne of Grace, so that we may receive mercy and find Grace to help in our time of need.

—Hebrews 4:16

So that in the ages to come He might show the surpassing riches of His Grace in kindness towards us in Christ Jesus.

— Ephesians 2:7

As a Christian, you spend a lot of time learning about grace. You learn how unmerited grace is. How precious grace is. We sing about amazing grace. And you learn the importance or giving grace here on earth to each other.

Let me be clear about this: in no way am I comparing earthly grace with God's grace. While we are charged to show grace as grace has been extended to us, we aren't even in the same ballgame with God's grace. That being said, I do want to share with you some examples of kindness I have experienced that have given me an earthly taste of grace.

When you royally mess up, you crave grace and forgiveness from those you've hurt. You look for it in any shape, form, or fashion. And let me tell you something, it makes your day when you find it. You try not to read too much into these little things, and you have to remind yourself that things aren't okay. But when you get this far down, little things mean a great deal when you receive them.

Here're a few examples of that grace I would like to share:

A good friend who lost money called one day a few years ago and said that he wanted to help me sell lights. He even invited me to come out to his hometown and had me stay in his guest house for a few days! Do you realize how incredible that is? Someone who just took a hit, calls me up and says, "Come on out. Let's partner up and sell some lights." And that's what we did. Six years later, we are still at it. We talk daily and not just about business. For him to be able to put the past behind him and launch into a new venture is extremely gracious on his part.

I have a childhood friend that I couldn't pay back. He called one day and said, "Mouse (my old nickname), don't get me wrong, I'd like to be paid back but if that never happens, I want you to know that won't change things between you and me." I still get teary eyed when I recall that conversation. You can and should forgive people, but to go that extra mile meant so much to me then and now. We go to lunch occasionally, talk often, and have even traveled to ball games together. He has followed through on what he told me awhile back. Things haven't changed between us. That is a strong testament to how he views the importance of forgiveness.

I mentioned earlier being a founding member of a bank that took a big loss. The banker, his staff, and my fellow board members all treated me extremely well throughout all this mess. One by one, as I would see them out, I would receive a firm handshake and a warm smile. I don't know if I'm forgiven or not, but they made me feel that way and that means so much.

This may seem very small to you, but to me it was huge. One of my bankers and I were serving on a countywide board together. Things were falling apart, and the bank knew the score. I wasn't far from resigning from the board. As I was attending my final meeting, we had a meal. The banker, a very strong Christian, asked me to say the blessing before we ate. For him to extend me that honor in the midst of what was going on behind the scenes was very gracious.

A third banker is a fellow I go to church with; we were even in a small group together. He, no doubt, felt betrayed. Throughout all this, he always greeted me with a smile and warm handshake. One night a couple of years ago, we were both at a community event and bumped into each other in a hallway. We spoke and shook hands. He said, "Hey, let me buy you a beer." He did and I texted him the next day and told him that that was the best beer I had ever had ... and I meant it.

My best friend from college took a hit and has remained a true friend throughout it all. It's ironic in the fact that, from the outside looking in, he does not have the appearance of a devout church going man. However, the grace he has extended to me is remarkable and an example that all Christians would/should admire. Sure, he wants to be paid back and we both look forward to that day, but that elephant in the room doesn't stop him from being one of my best friends on earth. It takes a lot for someone to be able to put bad circumstances aside and treat you well. I have experienced much more of that than I deserve.

Little things mean so much. A text at Christmastime or on your birthday. A handshake. A smile and nod across a room. When you have caused so much hurt, you look for every sign of forgiveness available. When you run across one it means so much.

As I mentioned earlier, my sister Susan's inheritance took a major hit. She was hurt and rightfully so. She was upset and wanted answers, but there were no good answers. I sought her forgiveness and, being the strong Christian she is, she assured me I was forgiven. She could have left it right there and been justified, but she didn't. She has continued to stay in touch and done more than her part to restore a broken relationship. I can't tell you how much it means to me to have a sister that cherishes a relationship beyond the hurt I caused.

My wife Julie. I could write several chapters on the grace she has extended to me. However, being a private person, she wouldn't let me do that. In the earlier chapters, I told you how badly I hurt her. With that in mind, the fact we are still married is a profound example of her graciousness.

When things blew up, my oldest daughter asked if she was going to ask for a divorce. Her answer was simple yet resolute: "No, I married for better or worse and this is by far the worst, but I'm not going anywhere." That's not just grace, that is resilience at its best. Every day throughout this storm has been a show of grace on her part. No one would have blamed her, least of all me, had she left.

I remember Julie's college roommates came to visit for a couple of days to give her support. They were really good girls who have each had storms of their own to contend with. One had a sister who was an attorney who said that in most cases like this, the marriage does not survive. They were trying to prepare Julie for the worst and let her know that they were there for her no matter what. They were very well meaning, but that in and of itself could have given the push to make a hard move and walk away.

Julie's grace abounds. Her commitment to our wedding vows shows our married children that marriage is for keeps ... that those words "for better or worse" mean something. I could write so much more but I better stop right there.

Being in a small town, my storm has a lot of similarities with a divorce. Because of my actions, I became "separated" from some of my friends. I fully understand. Being around me was unsettling. I'm toxic. The people I hurt financially—and we had many mutual friends—put folks in a hard spot.

It used to be your town
It used to be my town, too
You never know 'til it all falls down
Somebody loves you
Somebody loves you

—James Taylor

I appreciate the friends who didn't have a dog in the fight who aren't ashamed to call me a friend, publicly and privately. Most would prefer to appear neutral, and I fully understand. I really do. Being seen with me can be viewed as condoning my actions. People willing to do that can be deemed guilty by association. I have friends with high standing in the community that have put their own reputations (and client base) at risk by unashamedly being my friend.

I don't judge anyone who wishes to avoid the appearance of remaining my friend. If there is a divide, I caused it and I accept full responsibility. But, since this chapter is on grace received, I did want to let you know that people who accept me, warts and all, mean the world to me. Their friendship to me comes at a cost and with risks.

An interesting side bar: One person who did lose money kept close contact but didn't want anyone to know that we were still friends. We would still go eat lunch, but it always had to be out of town and he cautioned me to not tell anyone. Fair enough. His grace came with a string attached, but hey, I'll take whatever I can get. It's all undeserved but appreciated.

Let me bring this back around to the real lesson. In an earthly sense, I have craved and appreciated grace to its fullest. This storm has brought me to a greater understanding of how precious it is. It has given me just a faint glimmer of how precious God's Grace is. How unmerited it is. I don't deserve any grace from the people hurt in my storm. Furthermore, and most importantly, none of us deserve an ounce of God's Grace. That is what is so amazing about it!

Amazing grace how sweet the sound
That saved a wretch like me
I once was lost, but now I'm found
Was blind but now I see

I have lived through an earthly financial bankruptcy. I had a debt too large for me to pay. We all must come to grips with the fact that we are spiritually bankrupt. Our sins, large and small, put us in a place where we must admit our debt is too much to overcome on our own. We must file spiritual bankruptcy (confess our sins). We must acknowledge that there is someone willing to release us from our debts (Jesus Christ). We must accept His offer to wipe away our debt (receive His Salvation). Then we must turn from the things that caused our debt (repent).

Once we have done that, we forever have a Redeemer willing to grant us grace when we fail. Grace of this nature is the most expensive and precious available. It cost God His only Son. It cost Jesus His Life on a cross on Calvary. The Father and Son did this just for you. Of all the lessons in this book—of all the lessons you can ever be exposed to—this is the one that means the most. At the end of the day, it's the only one that truly matters!

Application:

Have you declared spiritual bankruptcy? If not, please do so today! Pray to God that you acknowledge that you are a sinner and that you want Him to save you by His Son Jesus's blood on the cross. Tell Him you want to turn from your sins and follow Him. Tell Him you want to receive the power He has to offer, then go tell a friend or two what you just did!

Lesson 4

Praise God in the Storm and for the Storm!

About midnight Paul and Silas were praying and singing hymns to God, and the prisoners were listening to them.

—Acts 16:25

But the Lord was with Joseph and showed him steadfast love and gave him favor in the sight of the keeper of the prison.

—Genesis 39:21

And we know that for those who love God all things work together for good, for those who are called according to his purpose.

—Romans 8:28

There are things that you can never experience in a life lived on a mountain top. For that reason alone, we should praise God in our storms. While in that valley, if we earnestly pray for God to be glorified by His standards, then things start to make sense.

Please don't get me wrong. It's hard to get to that point. Human nature wants relief, and we want it now. However, physical relief from our circumstances shortstops the work God is doing for us and through us. That's why I am writing this book. I want you to get to know me, get to know my storm, and most of all to know my source of strength and peace. When that happens, then God will be glorified, and I can praise Him all the more in my valley.

Praising God in a storm and for a storm is a learned response that you can't experience without the aid of the Holy Spirit. You have to pray daily (and throughout the day) for Him to walk with you, grant you Peace, and bring you understanding and opportunities to learn and serve.

Salvation comes in an instant, and sanctification takes a lifetime and is never reached this side of Heaven. However, if we are intentional in our walk, we can look back from time to time and see how we have progressed. Here is how I progressed in this one instance.

First, I started praising God in my storm and for my storm, even though I didn't feel it at first. That's not really a requirement. Much of my walk and maturing starts off with "doing it" then later "feeling." God knows our heart and knows when that transition takes place.

Next, I moved to asking that God be glorified by my storm, which was a natural progression in praising Him.

Finally, I added that I wanted God to be glorified by His standards and not mine. That is the toughest part because you open yourself up to going wherever God leads you. You end up being compelled by the Holy Spirit to do things like writing a book. A book that tells the whole world how you messed up in hopes someone out there sees something in you that they want and need. Jesus.

When you praise God in a storm, it opens the door for His peace to come in. Withholding praise will shortstop the peace that passes all understanding. I have mentioned previously my friend who lost his son at age twenty-one. He shared with me that in the months following his son's death, praising God in his loss was the only thing that brought him relief from his grief.

In the previous chapter, I gave examples of grace here on earth that I've experienced. That's cause to praise God. I would not have chosen to live out this storm, but if I had had my way, I would have missed out on all those blessings.

God sees our big picture and we don't. We have no idea how our storm fits into God's plan for our life unless we trust Him and consequently praise Him for our storm. It could be that God knew I had a character flaw that would have cost me dearly had I been wildly successful as a car dealer. Something that riches might have exposed that lead me to bad choices, choices that could've cost me all the things that I hold dear. We all know what that looks like. Men succeed in business and become "Teflon." At the end of their lives, some end up sad and all alone. Possibly, my humbling saved me from myself.

I remember a dealer meeting where my friend John Mitchell and I were sitting at a table with several very successful car men. There were ten of us dining together. Of the ten, John and I were the only ones with our original wives. Not saying that all these marriages ended because of the husband's overinflated ego, but that seems to be a factor in many. The prevenient grace God gives us in the form of a storm is something worthy of our praise!

In praising God in our trials, we yield to His understanding of what's best for us. No one with good sense plans a storm. But once you are in it, you better try and learn the lesson God has for you. Taking that posture, you receive those revelations and that is cause for great praise.

In my case, I don't see an end to my storm. I'm sixty-one years old and have a mountain of debt. If I chose not to praise God in my storm, then I effectively chose not to praise God.

Withholding praise to my God Almighty because of my circumstances is an inconceivable thought. We are made to praise our Creator in all things good and bad. When you are in a tough spot, you start thinking more about where your true relief lies. If you are saved by grace, then your rescue from this world is in Heaven. You yearn for that joy more when this old world gets heavy. When you start contemplating Heaven, praise is a natural response. Relief may never come here on earth, but we can rest assured it will come when we cross the River Jordan. That my friend is the most important reason of all to praise God!

Turn your eyes upon Jesus,
Look full in His wonderful face,
And the things of earth will grow strangely dim,
In the light of His glory and grace.

From a financial standpoint when you lose it all, you really start paying attention to what you have left. Which is what we are supposed to do in the first place, right? When the things of this world get stripped away, you cherish what's left in a whole new light. You savor the relationships that remain and, most importantly, your relationship with Jesus Christ. Your joy comes from things money can't buy. The beauty of nature, sunsets, and sunrises. Love of your family. The opportunity to worship and serve in your church. It is cause for praise when you realize that the most important things in life aren't really things at all.

By the world's standards, I have lost. The other side is simply running out the clock. I praise God that that designation is not the end of my story. You see, just because I lost it all financially does not mean I have lost it all. I still have a chance to win if I am obedient to God in this storm and allow Him to use me. I have a real chance to tell my story and make a difference in someone else's life. That opportunity is something to celebrate! And whenever you have an opportunity to celebrate, is that not a reason to Praise God?

Application:

What blessing from God am I overlooking because of the distractions of this world? How can I become more deliberate in separating myself from the world and focus on praising God? How can I find God's purpose for the storm in my life and use it to glorify Him?

Lesson 5

God's Sustaining Grace is Available and Essential for Survival

Nevertheless, I tell you the truth; It is expedient for me to go away: for if I go not away, the Comforter will not come unto you: but if I depart, I will send Him unto you.

—John 16:7-14

But He said unto me, 'My Grace is sufficient for you, for my power is made perfect in weakness.' Therefore, I will boast all the more gladly of weakness, so that the power of Christ may rest upon me.

—2 Corinthians 12:9

Originally, I was going to do a chapter on both sustaining grace and the Holy Spirit, but the further I got into it, the more I realized I could not separate the two. They are too intertwined. The Holy Spirit is the conduit that delivers the grace that carries us through the hard times.

Every morning as I pray, I thank God for the gift of His Son on the cross and the gift of His Holy Spirit. I ask Him to grant me forgiveness for my past, hope for my future, and peace for my present, through the Blood and through the Spirit. Those are "spiritual" aspects of what I receive. Later I will talk about the miracles I'm blessed with of a tangible nature.

When you pray to be blessed with forgiveness, hope, and peace you must include the Holy Spirit in the equation. That is how you are allowed to experience those things. You pray for the Spirit to guide your thoughts, taking away the lies from Satan. There is an old saying that applies to all our thoughts, "You can't stop the birds from flying over your head, but you can stop them from making a nest in your hair." When you ask the Holy Spirit to guide your thoughts, you are asking Him to whisk away worry, shame, and despair and replace it with hope, forgiveness, and peace. Like so much of our journey, this too is a learned response. When I find myself dwelling in a place I don't belong, I try to snap back by saying, "Get thee behind me, Satan," and try to replace those thoughts immediately with positive thoughts.

Let me tell you something, Satan does not want you to have those things. When you are out of hope and peace, you are completely out of the game. He has you right where he wants you. Completely ineffective. However, when others see you surviving in a storm, they get to see God being glorified. Hopefully, they see that you have something that they want or want more of. That "something" is a manifestation of God's sustaining grace.

I have had people aware of my financial failure who are puzzled that I can remain positive and appear happy. Several people have asked me, "Did you ever consider just picking up and moving away to avoid all the shame?" More than one person has told me that they admire the fact that I didn't take my life.

In all three of those scenarios above, what people are really asking is, "How are you able to survive?" What they are really seeing is the sustaining grace of the Almighty God.

That is what this book is all about. My sharing the heartache and weakness allows God to show His strength. He tells us that

His strength is manifested in our weakness. Human nature says run and hide. When that happens, we rob God of an opportunity to be glorified.

During my collapse and bankruptcy, I can't tell you how many times I was embroiled in utter chaos and strife and breathed the short prayer, "Peace, Lord, peace, grant me peace in this moment." The circumstances didn't immediately change but my countenance always did. Calm clarity entered my being when I invited the Holy Spirit to take control of my emotions.

Contrary to popular belief, God will let you experience "more than you can handle." However, He won't give you more than HE can handle. His sustaining grace is there for us. I experience it daily and you can too! I promise.

As mentioned earlier, my bankruptcy plan called for me to pay around six thousand dollars per month, and I also had to keep my household up. Consequently, I needed God's help in a very practical way. God continues to bless me daily in that regard. I'd like to share with you some of the miracles I have been blessed to experience.

The fact that I'm close to satisfying my bankruptcy obligations is a miracle in itself. For thirty-five years, the car business was all I knew. I needed a job. Yet as I prayed for direction, I was led to call Joey Gilliland and ask him if he needed any help.

I didn't even know for sure what he did, but I knew he was successful at it. The lighting business was just an offshoot from his main business, but an incredible opportunity for me. God nudged me through that door and has richly blessed me ever since.

I believe that God also nudged Joey to take a chance on me. Joey is a strong believer and has invested himself in countless people who needed a second chance. Most cases involve addiction and the work environment he has provided for those folks has saved many lives. While my case didn't involve addiction, I would say I was probably about as toxic as anyone he has ever helped. I owe Joey and his brother Jason so much for befriending me and giving me an opportunity.

I'm a lighting contractor, but basically, I sell and sub out the installation process. Ultimately, I'm responsible for how things go, but my key role is finding a project and making a sale. In this line of work there is no safety net. If you don't sell, you don't eat.

And He said to them, 'Cast the net on the right side of the boat, and you will find *some.*' So they cast, and now they were not able to draw it in because of the multitude of fish.

—John 21:6

Every day, I pray that the Holy Spirit would show me where to fish and warm hearts in front of me. God has done just that time and time again. God has blessed me much like he did the Israelites with manna. Just what you need for today and today alone. In doing so, He has reminded me that He is my sustenance, my sustaining grace.

When we started selling lights, Joey had an inside in the poultry industry and I had connections in the car business. Consequently, I didn't have to make any cold calls. Same is true today. We have stayed busy week after week with referrals and introductions. Just like manna, the projects don't pile up waiting on me. They come about in a succession that only God can arrange. He has taught me to be at peace with that. He has allowed each yes I hear to be viewed as the miracle that it is. He is sustaining me in a very real way and teaching me to be at peace and rely on Him.

Here are some ways I have been blessed by God's sustaining Grace.

Coming out of Woods and Water in Tuscaloosa one day I bumped into a friend I haven't seen in twenty years. He introduced me to a friend of his who was a car dealer and two weeks later we were redoing his lot.

I had a casual conversation with a neighbor who worked in a family-run nursing home. Within a month, we were relighting that nursing home and their pharmacy. They then introduced me to someone at the local electric co-op, which led to their lights, six bank locations, another pharmacy, and another nursing home, all from a chance meeting and an "oh, by the way" question.

One of my installers was eating lunch one day and ran into an old client of his who worked at a major plant in the area. He found out they were looking at lights, and two weeks later, we were installing new lights at a massive plant.

I was introduced to a gentleman who used to be an electrical contractor but was in failing health. He offered to introduce me to his friend who was responsible for facilities at a major airport. That was several years ago, and I have been doing projects there ever since.

I could go on and on, but you get the picture. My life is a series of sustaining miracles. Yours may very well be too if you slow down and think about it. A buddy of mine is a strong Christian and a real estate broker. I asked him one day if he can look back on his career and see God's hand in it. He replied, "Oh yes!" I had a chance meeting with a man who owns a great deal of land in this county and who, for some reason, took a liking to me. That one relationship has made all the difference in the world to my career. I believe it was God who put him in my path.

I jokingly told him that my life in the lighting business has been a lot like the old video game *Frogger*. If you recall, the frog had to jump from log to log with the logs moving in different directions. If a log didn't come along at the right time, he disappeared off the screen and it was "game over." I praise God for the logs He has sent my way that have prevented me from disappearing off the screen!

I understand that my bankruptcy obligations are a small piece of my overall debt; however, it is something that I have to get through before I could start working on the other part.

We must have the Holy Spirit at the core of our existence if we are to survive a storm. If I didn't intentionally enlist Him in my daily life, I would be toast. Daily I pray for fresh anointing of the Holy Spirit ... asking Him to guide my thoughts, my actions, my communications, my decisions, my energy, and focus. That He would show me others in need of God's love and touch, that He would inspire and equip me to be of service in the Kingdom.

It is hard to do with all the noise in our lives, but we have to get still and get quiet to hear what God is trying to tell us. As I mentioned earlier, I listen to a devotion every morning from Wisdom Hunters.

Sidebar:
The head of Wisdom Hunters is Boyd Bailey. Boyd and I went to high school together and recently reconnected when I called to tell him about this book. I strongly recommend incorporating these devotions into your daily walk. I've been doing so for eight years now, and they have greatly enriched my life.

Back to my illustration/point. When I'm in my truck, going down the highway, out in the world, the volume on my phone has to be full blast to hear the message. Conversely, in my office at home in the morning, my volume setting is near zero so as not to wake anyone else in the house. That is a real-world metaphor for how we have to shut out the world to hear what the Holy Spirit has to share with us.

If you feel like God is giving you more than you can handle, you are probably right. At that point, it's time to hand it all over to God and pray to receive His sustaining grace. Remember, His strength is manifested in our weakness. Enlist the Holy Spirit into your storm and begin to experience that peace that passes all understanding.

Application:

How can I practically structure my day to keep the Holy Spirt involved at every point? How can I examine my life to regularly be aware of God's sustaining grace?

Lesson 6

Don't Let Satan Wreck Your Service or Witness

You intended to harm me, but God intended it for good to accomplish what is now being done, the saving of many lives.

—Genesis 50:20

Goal number one for Satan is to win your soul. If that is out of reach, his next best move is to take you out of the game and put you on the sidelines so you are no longer effective in your witness for Christ. We've all seen this before. Infidelity, addiction, greed, pride ... whatever our weakness, Satan can strike good men and women and cripple their witness.

His intentions are to shame us out of service, despite our level of repentance. Whenever we start to feel reconciliation and restoration he's right there, quick to remind us of our failure. Satan is the great accuser; Christ is our great Advocate. Christ takes our petition before God Almighty and tells Him we are worthy to be forgiven. God forgives and forgets. He separates us from our sin as far as east is from the west and remembers it no more.

If we allow a repented sin to define us, then we are in essence telling our Savior that His sacrifice for us fell short. His blood was insufficient to cover our sins. I think that's a dangerous place to be in.

We are told in the scriptures that we will be forgiven by the same measure that we forgive others. We covered that in a previous lesson; however, what if we took that one step further? By what measure do we forgive ourselves? He insists that we forgive ourselves so He can use us.

Think back on Peter. Full of courage, Peter told Christ that he would die right alongside Him! Shortly thereafter, he denied he even knew Jesus. That passage hurts me to read because I think I identify too much with it. Bold in the moment but shrink back later when the rubber meets the road. But how does that story end? Jesus gives Peter a chance to affirm his love three times (which Peter does) and instructs him to go and be in service for the Kingdom. Jesus said clearly, you made a mistake. I forgive you. Now get to work. Christ built His church upon a man who denied him in his very presence.

How does this all play out in our everyday life? I have viewed much of my struggle as spiritual warfare. Discerning spiritual warfare can be difficult; however, if we don't attempt to do so, then we have already lost.

Some things that happen are just life and we can't assign too much credit to Satan. But as Christians, it's imperative that we examine our lives to the point that we understand the battle at hand, understand the tests we are encountering, and the lessons to be learned. Old saying goes, an unexamined life ain't worth livin'!

In the midst of the battle, Satan can cut your witness off at the knees and render you broken, unable to confidently be a leader and a witness. That's exactly what happened to me. It might be where you find yourself right now. Wanting to do work for the Kingdom but letting Satan keep you on the sidelines.

No matter where we find ourselves, God is standing ready to assist us and give us an avenue of service. I mentioned earlier, before my fall, I held many offices in my church: finance chairman, trustee chairman, capital funds campaign chairman, administrative board chairman, and head of the staff parish relations committee for seven years.

I felt I had some gifts regarding communication and leadership. I tried to use those gifts for the good of the Kingdom. When I "fell from grace," all that was over. I knew that anything I was associated with would meet with extra scrutiny and rightfully so.

Consequently, I shrunk back into the shadows and became more of an attendee. Thankfully, my faith never wavered but I felt like I had lost my chance to lead and witness. Everything I did in life was framed off what the people I hurt would think. Satan knew me well. How do you kill off a "people pleaser"? Put him in a situation that he can't reconcile, and he is toast.

I felt like no one wanted to hear anything I had to say. The sins of my past took that platform away. The Bible is clear that leaders should be chosen from those who "kept their own house in order." From a financial standpoint, my "house" was burned to the ground. Game over.

But my God and my Savior said, "Not so fast, I have plans for you." Plans that would put me in a position of service that I could not have assumed without a collapse. This book and my testimony are a result of my pain.

If you are willing to tell Satan to get behind you, you can begin to live out your faith in sight of others who need to see it. You might be restored to a position similar to your past or possibly something completely different. Either way, it all starts with obedience.

Our God is a God of great turnarounds. However, those turnarounds come as a result of obedience. Obedience starts with repentance. Once there is repentance, we have to actively pursue guidance from the Holy Spirit as to which direction our turnaround should go.

As you start down that road of restoration, be aware that it's not easy. There is a lion that waits to steal, kill, and destroy. However, the One who walks with us is the great Overcomer! He has plans to prosper us and use us for His Kingdom.

This is important: Once you own your past, it can't own you anymore. Once you step out of the shadows, you are free to move forward. The truth does, indeed, set you free.

The real "truth" is that you are a child of the Most High God Almighty and He wants a relationship with you no matter what. No matter what you have done, he has a job for you to do. Think of it this way, there are sheep that will go hungry if you don't feed them as instructed.

Do you ever see a scar on someone and wonder how they got it? If we step out and let folks see our scars, then that opens the door for our stories. Our stories are our testimony. Our testimony points others to Christ and, in doing so, we feed the sheep.

I'm not proud of the fact that so many people were hurt as I acquired my scars. It grieves me greatly. However, my scars are here for all to see. Now, my lessons learned are too.

I pray that the things I have shared in this book make a difference to someone struggling along life's highway. I hope that one day someone will read this and share with me the lessons they have learned as well. It is sweet to know that we serve a God who won't cast us aside when we fail.

My prayer is that God will be glorified by me sharing this … that someone out there will want to experience the sustaining grace that I've come to know so intimately through this storm.

My storm, My Savior. His grace truly is sufficient for all our trials. Amen!

Application:

What area of Kingdom service is calling me out of the shadows?

Lesson 7

We Have an Identity and Job in Christ

As the people were in expectation, and all were questioning in their hearts concerning John, whether he might be the Christ, John answered them all, saying, 'I baptize you with water, but he who is mightier than I is coming, the strap of whose sandals I am not worthy to untie. He will baptize you with the Holy Spirit and fire. His winnowing fork is in his hand, to clear his threshing floor and to gather the wheat into his barn, but the chaff he will burn with unquenchable fire.'

So with many other exhortations he preached good news to the people. But Herod the tetrarch, who had been reproved by him for Herodias, his brother's wife, and for all the evil things that Herod had done, added this to them all, that he locked up John in prison.

Now when all the people were baptized, and when Jesus also had been baptized and was praying, the heavens were opened, and the Holy Spirit descended on him in bodily form, like a dove; and a voice came from heaven, 'You are my beloved Son; with you I am well pleased.'

—Luke 3:15-22

This chapter isn't necessarily born out of my financial fall but instead a two-part lesson that can be best summed up by lines from two great songs:

"Happiness ain't just for high achievers."

—Brooks and Dunn

"I love to tell the story of unseen things above, of Jesus and His Glory, of Jesus and His love."

—Fischer and Hanley

In the fall of 2022, my wife Julie and I finally got to attend a parents' weekend with our son Sam at the United States Naval Academy. Sam is in his third year; however, the previous parents' weekends were casualties of Covid-19. The idea behind these events is to allow parents an inside look at their midshipmen's daily life on the yard. Also, there are opportunities to meet other parents and forge new relationships.

One of the mothers organized a cluster of parents comprised of Sam's four best friends. This truly was a remarkable group of kids and their parents. The group of dads contained the following: an Ivy League educated NYC architect, a former Marine pilot (who is now an FBI agent), a young retiree who was an ultra-distance cyclist, and a USNA grad who was an IT director for a Fortune 500 firm. They were all in their forties or early fifties and at the top of their game.

Then there's me! A sixty-one-year-old, used-up car dealer thirty pounds overweight with a bum ankle and a pacemaker. I was a fish out of water. I've been in that spot many times before. Usually, it was around high-roller car dealers whose sole intent was to make sure you knew how rich and important they were. I think the term is "me monster"—what I've got, what I've done, where I've been, etc.—blah, blah, blah!

The difference in this instance, as opposed to previous ones, was that all the guys mentioned above were really good people. They were humble and made me feel very much at home. The impressive things about them that I learned were pulled out in genuine conversation, not proclaimed in an effort to impress anyone. They were interested in getting to know me and explored my interests. The "fish out of water" feelings were 100 percent on my end, not anything imposed by my new friends. I enjoyed their company, and they left me somewhat inspired to do better.

My inadequate feelings were based in my regret for not living a more disciplined life, not taking better care of myself, not pursuing meaningful things and mastering them. In a nutshell, not being all I could be.

That Sunday morning, I snuck out of the room and went for a drive. Said my prayers, listened to my morning devotion, and contemplated my feelings of wanting to "do better." I hoped that the next time I saw these guys that they might see a better version of me.

Later that morning, Julie, Sam, and I went to the USNA Chapel for the Protestant worship service. The chapel is one of the most beautiful buildings I have ever been in. It was awe inspiring to say the least. As I sat there quietly before the service, my feelings of inadequacy seemed to melt away. I felt at home. The service started and I knew every song: "Rock of Ages," "His Eye is on the Sparrow," and "Amazing Grace," which brought me to tears. I couldn't sing the last verse because I was so choked up! That thundering pipe organ and a congregation singing:

When we've been there ten thousand years, bright
shining as the sun,
We've no less days to sing God's Praise than when
we first begun.

You see, inside that chapel, I didn't see myself as an underachiever.
I was a child of the Most High. Saved by His Grace, washed in
His Blood. I belonged. That day, I fully understood the meaning
of that old saying, "The ground at the foot of the Cross is level."

I was so thankful to be reminded of that fact. Sure, I need
to do better in lots of personal areas in my life, but the most
important thing I need to reflect on is how inspiring was my
faith to my new friends? Did I do anything intentional to point
my new friends toward my Jesus? Did they see something in me
that made them want to know more about my faith? This brings
me to the second part of my lesson learned. Our faith must be
on display.

You see, everyone you meet falls into one of two spiritual
categories:

They need something you have (Jesus),
or ...
You need something they have (insight into their walk).

We as Christians need to be keenly aware of this. It's our job. It's
the Great Commission. I'm not preaching to you, I'm preaching
to me! I fail miserably at being intentional about sharing my
faith. I think in part, that shortcoming pushed me to write this
book ... to somehow erase years of being shy about my faith in
one fell swoop. All laid out there for the world to see/read.

The story I shared points up my human deficiency of
looking inward toward my personal qualities and not taking up

my identity in Christ. That is a phrase I have heard all my life. Find your identity in Christ. I think I'm starting to understand that a little better. My relationship with Christ should be the most defining thing about me. In a big way, that concept is very freeing. Get that right and everything else either takes care of itself or doesn't really matter.

Let me tell you a quick story ...

I used to live close to a fellow named Doyle. Doyle was a nice looking guy who didn't work and walked everywhere he went. I would occasionally pick him and give him a ride home. He would always ask for a few dollars when I let him out. Doyle had a wife and son and lived in a house without indoor plumbing. Our Sunday school class pitched in one year and built a kitchen/bathroom onto the house. They were very appreciative but were never very motivated to get jobs or break out of their poverty.

Doyle eventually ended up with a car, which expanded his circle of panhandling. If you ever got tired of Doyle coming around, just offer him a job and he would disappear for a while. He was a very interesting character. He wasn't wired quiet right, but he wasn't a con man by any stretch of the imagination. What you see is what you get. He just didn't have the wherewithal to hold down a job.

One day Doyle was in my office telling me about an incident where a man was getting on him about being lazy and was talking rough to him. He said something I will never forget: "I'm not a worthless piece of trash. I'm a son of the Most High God, I'm an heir to His Kingdom, and God loves me." Doyle found his identity in Christ, not his many shortcomings. Doyle was a simple man with a very profound understanding of who he was. I don't endorse his way of life but at the end of the day, I do admire how he found his identity in Christ and that was sufficient.

We need to make sure that the people we encounter know who and whose we are. Putting that in the forefront is a must for it opens so many doors. It allows us to share Jesus and allows God to use the people in our path to teach us new truths, to inspire us to be better followers. Burying our identity shortstops so many things.

A friend and mentor of mine from church gave a devotion over thirty years ago that made a great point. Are you a shoe salesman who is a Christian or a Christian shoe salesman? The difference lies in the answer to an oft asked question, "What do you do?" If your answer is "I sell shoes," then you are a shoe salesman and maybe or maybe not a Christian. If your answer is "Well, I'm a follower of Jesus Christ, but selling shoes is how I support my habit, then you see yourself as a Christian first and what you do is secondary."

You might say that the illustration above is all about schematics, but the truth lies in how we really see ourselves ... where do we draw our identity from? Our occupation or our role in the Kingdom. Keeps going back to the concept of "dying to self to live in Christ." Not easy but definitely worth striving for!

We need people in our lives who require something from us. And we need to bring something to the table as well. Those guys I met that weekend inspired me. Sadly, I left on the sidelines the most important thing I had to offer. I should have woven my faith into our conversations. Not in an aggressive manner but in an intentional way that left them knowing more about me and the importance of Christ in my life.

Missed opportunities are not totally lost if they serve as motivation for future encounters. That's where I am right now. I'm motivated to be intentional in sharing my faith. I recently went through a study by Mark Mittelberg titled "Contagious Faith." It's a great study that helps you identify your witnessing "style" and offers practical ways to share your faith. Studies like this are great, but only if we put them into practice. I'm committed to doing just that. Most importantly, I am inviting the Holy Spirit to guide me in my endeavor. Asking Him to point out people in need of what I have. Asking Him to inspire and equip me for service in the Kingdom.

In closing, I'm thankful that "happiness ain't just for high achievers" and I'm thankful to be newly motivated to "tell the story of Jesus and His love."

Application:

Prepare yourself daily for encounters that lead to an opportunity to do work for the Kingdom of God.

Postscript: Closing Thoughts

November 1, 2022

As I write this final chapter, it is with a great deal of humility and joy I share that I have a contract on my desk from a publishing company. Someone out there believes that this story is compelling enough to put it into print. That in and of itself is a miracle and evidence of God's hand in this storm and project. I have never viewed this book as an end unto itself, but instead a tool to be used in helping other people find Jesus and what He has to offer. To be one step closer to that ideal is very exciting. Our God is a God of great turnarounds and irony. I have gone from trying my best to shroud my story in shame and secrecy to praying for a platform to tell the world.

Something truly amazing happened between finishing Lesson 7 and when I sent my manuscript off. Julie was once again reading *The Advertiser Gleam* and saw an article about a friend of mine who had gotten into some financial trouble in a neighboring county.

I knew nothing of what she told me and was saddened to hear the news. However, I found myself in a unique position to help. My friend was exactly who the Holy Spirit had in mind when he prompted me to write this book. Prior to this project, my message to my friend would've been very benign. Something along the lines of "Praying for you buddy. Let me know if I can help." Nice enough but not really much help.

However, now having my story in a written format, I was able to offer my friend much more. I was able to share my manuscript with him and show him how my Jesus could make a difference in his daily life. Because of my storm and being compelled to share it, I was able to actually minister to him. It felt so good! I feel like it was God giving me a small glimpse into what might lie ahead.

Previously I shared that I was going to start a ledger, listing in the front all the people I hurt. After that, I hope to list the names of those that are helped by sharing this hurt and God's grace in it. My friend in Jackson County has become the first name on that new list. Hopefully, one day, the new list will surpass the old list and God can be glorified by His standards.

If in fact you found something in these pages that has helped you understand the nature of what God has to offer, I would love to hear about it. Please send me a note at stevemoultrie@gmail.com. Also, if you are part of a group that would like me to come share my story in person, please let me know that as well. I would love to.

In closing, thanks for letting me tell my story to you. May God bless you as you journey along life's highway and know you are never alone!

Yours in Christ,
Steve

Review Requested:

We'd like to know if you enjoyed the book.
Please consider leaving a review on the platform
from which you purchased the book.

CPSIA information can be obtained
at www.ICGtesting.com
Printed in the USA
LVHW101134140323
741587LV00006B/824

9 781682 358030